D0408342

CONVERSATIONS ON THERAPY

BOOKS BY JAY HALEY

Strategies of Psychotherapy, Second Edition
Problem-Solving Therapy, Second Edition
Power Tactics of Jesus Christ, Second Edition
Conversations with Milton H. Erickson, M.D. (three volumes)
Ordeal Therapy
Reflections on Therapy and Other Essays
Leaving Home
Uncommon Therapy: The Psychiatric Techniques of Milton H. Erickson, M.D.
Changing Families (editor)
Advanced Techniques of Hypnosis and Therapy: The Selected Papers of Milton H. Erickson, M.D. (editor)
Techniques of Family Therapy (with Lynn Hoffman)

AUDIOTAPES BY JAY HALEY

In His Own Voice: Milton H. Erickson, M.D. (four audiotapes)
The First Therapy Session: How to Interview Clients and Identify Problems Successfully

A NORTON PROFESSIONAL BOOK

CONVERSATIONS ON THERAPY

*Popular Problems
and Uncommon Solutions*

David R. Grove
Jay Haley

W. W. NORTON & COMPANY
NEW YORK   LONDON

Printed in the United States of America.

First Edition

The text of this book was composed in 11/13 Janson. Composition by Bytheway Typesetting Services, Inc. Manufacturing by Haddon Craftsmen.
Book design by Justine Burkat Trubey

Library of Congress Cataloging-in-Publication Data

Grove, David R.
    Conversations on therapy / David R. Grove and Jay Haley.
        p.   cm.
    "A Norton publication book"–Ser. t.p.
    Includes bibliographical references.
    ISBN 0-393-70155-7
    1. Family psychotherapy–Case studies.   I. Haley, Jay.
II. Title.
    [DNLM: 1. Family Therapy–methods.   WM 430.5.F2 G883c   1993]
RC488.5.G764   1993
616.89'156–dc20
DNLM/DLC   92-48451   CIP
for Library of Congress

W.W. Norton & Company, Inc., 500 Fifth Avenue, New York, N.Y. 10110
W.W. Norton & Company, Ltd., 10 Coptic Street, London WC1A 1PU

1 2 3 4 5 6 7 8 9 0

CONTENTS

          No Desire for Sex   135
          Amnesia   147
          Two Stories   157
          Can One Personality Be Enough?   181

      NOTES   199
      INDEX   201

ACKNOWLEDGMENTS

WITH MANY OF THE families in this book I (DRG) was the primary therapist; however, in four examples I was supervising the therapy live from behind a one-way-mirror. I would like to acknowledge the therapists in these cases, who invited me to work with them and skillfully executed interventions that were helpful to the families. The therapists were Pamela Cibik, Karen Grider, Marilyn Hartline and David Miller. I would also like to thank "Karen" (her true name is being withheld to protect her confidentiality) for allowing me to include her story in this book. Although all names, characteristics and identifying details of the families in this book have been altered to protect their confidentiality, the therapy descriptions and the conversations with Haley accurately reflect my work.

Many individuals have contributed to the actual making of this book. I would like to thank Karen Black for transcribing my tapes into a format usable on a computer. I would like to thank Patrick McKenry, Judith Eggers, and Patrick Early for reviewing the manuscript and providing helpful feedback. I would like to especially thank Cloé Madanes in this regard, since her comments inspired me to make major improvements on the original manuscript. I am also grateful to Susan Barrows Munro, who edited the book.

My most profound gratitude goes to Jay Haley, not only for agreeing to undertake this project and guiding me through it, but most of all for being a patient and generous teacher.

INTRODUCTION

PART ONE
by David Grove

THIS BOOK CONSISTS of a series of conversations between myself and Jay Haley. The conversations include entire case presentations, as well as excerpts from consultations. The cases selected for this book were chosen for several reasons. The families and the interventions discussed are interesting. More importantly, however, these cases represent what I consider to be a cross-section of those seen in mental health centers: a variety of problems, many of which are very serious and chronic in nature, with some threat of family dismemberment and several systems, such as the court and protective services, already involved with the family. Many of these cases represent the type of problems that threaten to burn out therapists. This book, therefore, offers ideas for handling these difficult situations.

After receiving several years of training with Jay Haley and Cloé Madanes at the Family Therapy Institute, I began meeting with Haley individually to consult about families with whom I was working both as a therapist and as a supervisor behind the mirror. This book is a collection of those conversations. The difficulty of the cases ranges from moderate to severe, with a variety of presenting problems being offered. When an entire case is presented, a description of the family and problem being brought to therapy, a transcript of the consultation with Haley, and a follow-up on the outcome of the case are offered. Where appropriate, a discussion section is also offered to clarify the rationale for the strategies used in the case. In addition to entire case presentations, excerpts from conversations are also offered; these describe a particular therapy procedure or raise a current issue in the field.

The purpose of the consultations was to devise a strategy for the particular family and problem being discussed. The book, therefore, is intended as a demonstration of the practical implementation of therapy with a variety of problems and circumstances. Although many of the therapeutic procedures outlined in this book have been discussed elsewhere, their essentials are exposed as Haley and I draw upon therapy as we know it and apply the ideas to these particular cases. We acknowledge that many of the ideas in this book have come from our readings and experiences and so from other therapists in the field who have offered ideas in the literature and at workshops.

Although the purpose of these conversations was to discuss particular cases, the reader will find theoretical issues clarified in the ways the cases were handled. The conversations also serve as examples of a specific model of supervision. The opportunity to talk about different ways of doing therapy resulted in discussions that went beyond the particular problem being presented.

Some of the interventions described here are unusual because in many cases I had already tried the more routine therapy procedures without success. I was looking for new ways to work with these difficult problems.

Finally, I would like to note that these are edited and not verbatim transcripts. Also, sections of our original conversations which were not relevant to the cases or issues being presented in this book were deleted.

PART TWO
by Jay Haley

THIS IS A BOOK of conversations largely about difficult cases. The goal of such conversations is to provide ways of thinking about problems and the interventions that might be used. I offer suggestions about what might be done, and Mr. Grove might or might not apply the ideas in his work with the family. With these kinds of case discussion, the consultant is not responsible for the outcome of the case—unlike live supervision where he or she can guide the therapist directly. What the consultant can do is make suggestions and allow the therapist to choose among them or ignore them. Of the three kinds of therapy supervision—live supervision, viewing videorecordings, and discussing the case—case discussions allow the participants the greatest range of conversation stimulated by the problems being presented. This type of consultation also most depends upon the ways the therapist describes the situation, since the consultant cannot see an interview. It helps if the therapist and consultant share a common language and think about cases in similar ways. That was so here, since David Grove had been in training with me as a therapist and supervisor for several years.

It may be a problem for some readers that the standard procedures of a strategic approach are not specifically presented here, because often Mr. Grove had tried those procedures before he brought the case for discussion. He was seeking new ways of thinking about the problem and new interventions since the routine procedures had not worked. As often happens, sometimes he overlooked an idea that would have been obvious to him in some other case.

The reader should not expect this to be a systematic training book. It is a book of conversations about therapy stimulated by some particular problem. It is not profound, but practical.

David Grove has done the work of this book. He selected the cases, brought them to me and described them, recorded our conversations, edited them into reasonably coherent English, and appended the follow-ups. I was free to offer him some ideas which I thought were relevant.

CONVERSATIONS ON THERAPY

1 | EMPOWERING FATHERS

A STEPFATHER WITH TWINS

THIS IS A CASE OF two twins who almost burned down their family's home. The twins, age 10, were not identical. One was average build. He was the "good" twin, the mother's favorite. The other twin was huge. He was overweight, looked older than his age, and was the family "troublemaker." The boys lived with their mother, stepfather, and baby sister. The stepfather worked in a low-paying job and the mother stayed home and cared for the boys.

The overall family picture for these boys was filled with strife. The mother divorced their biological father seven years prior to the therapy, but the man never accepted the divorce. He had sporadic contact with the boys, and when he appeared on the scene he harassed the mother about leaving him, and threatened physical violence with the stepfather.

The mother and stepfather struggled with each other on how to handle the boys, particularly the "troublemaker" twin. Violence was a serious problem. The typical sequence in this family went like this: The mother struggled to handle the "troublemaker" twin and kept the stepfather out. Eventually, she would ask the stepfather to help and the boy would get very upset about his stepfather's attempting to discipline him. The boy and stepfather then would escalate and become seriously violent with each other, with the boy breaking household items and attacking the stepfather. The mother would then become upset with the stepfather and he would again with-draw.

The mother's mother was also involved in this drama. The "trou-blemaker" twin was the grandmother's favorite. Anytime there was serious trouble the boy called his grandmother and she sided with him against the mother.

The family came to the attention of professionals after a very serious episode in which the family's house could have been burned down. The incident occurred on a weekend while both parents were away and the boys were being watched by a babysitter. The boys were playing and got in an argument. The babysitter intervened and sided with the "good" twin. The three argued and the fight escalated. The babysitter somehow locked the "troublemaker twin" in the ga-rage. He proceeded to pour gasoline all over, threatening to set the house on fire. His brother called the grandmother, who insisted on talking to the "troublemaker." The grandmother calmed the boy down and the house was saved.

When the mother got home she was so upset that she took the boys to protective services and requested counseling. Protective services' response was to remove both boys from the home and place them in a residential setting for nine months. When the boys were finally sent home, the family was referred to me for therapy, some-thing the mother had requested nine months earlier.

I immediately got a "no violence" agreement from the stepfather and began attempting to change the pattern between the mother and stepfather. I was only partially successful at that. I also wanted to include the grandmother in the therapy, but the mother was adamant about holding her out. Although the boys had improved and the violence at home was eliminated, at the time of this consultation the mother continued to be very depressed about the "whole family situation." The "troublemaker" twin was also having serious problems at school. He was placed in a special class for behavior problem children and was doing poorly in this environment. He was belliger-ent with the teacher daily, had gotten into several serious fights with other boys, had no friends at school, and had recently been thrown off the bus.

The consultation begins.

HALEY   What do the boys call their stepdad?

GROVE   They call him by his first name. With their biological dad it's unclear what they want. They say they're mad at him because he promises them things and then doesn't keep his promises.

HALEY   Well, you've got a complicated case. You've got the kids in a triangle with the biological father and mother, then also in a triangle with the stepfather and the mother, and also with the mother and grandmother. There's probably a triangle with the school and the family, and the residential program probably blamed the parents for the kids' problems as well. It's a matter of priority. Where do you start? Do you have a hypothesis on which triangle is the hottest?

GROVE   The hottest triangle is the mother, the son and the stepdad. One hypothesis would be that the problems keep the stepdad in the family. The mother worries about losing him, so I think she's incompetent with the boys as a way of giving her husband a purpose in the family. I'm not sure what exactly is going on between the mother, the grandmother and the kids. I don't have any idea what she says to the kids or to the mother.

HALEY   I'm sure she's blaming her daughter for the way the kids are behaving.

GROVE   On the biological dad, I have talked to the "troublemaker" alone about his dad.

HALEY   What does he say when he's alone?

GROVE   He says he's not interested in his biological dad. But he's obviously very hurt about his dad. It's a sensitive topic for him.

HALEY   Does he say why he's behaving the way he's behaving?

GROVE   He just presents himself like he wants his way and that is that. He does complain about his stepdad being too hard on him. I'm pretty sure the stepdad has stopped the violence though. I told the stepdad that if the boy starts breaking things, or if he comes at him like he's going to hit him, he was to wrestle the boy to the ground and hold him. Not hurt him, but just hold him until he's calmed down. The stepdad actually did that and that stopped the violence.

HALEY   The boy got the stepdad to demonstrate that he can restrain him.

GROVE   Right. There is serious trouble with the boy at school. Also, the mother says, "I'm depressed about the whole family situation." My plan is to have a school conference. One problem for the boy at school is that he sticks out like a sore thumb.

HALEY   He's a big fellow.

GROVE   He's very big yes.

HALEY   Fat?

GROVE   Fat, yes.

HALEY   The other twin isn't?

GROVE   No. The other twin is average build. You'd never guess they were twins.

HALEY   You know, twins present a special problem. It's usually with identical twins, but it could also happen here. They struggle to differentiate themselves and they work at being different from one another. Sometimes they struggle at having some feeling of being themselves. You see that with identical twins. They look alike, dress alike, go to the same class. Sometimes they develop a problem as a way to differentiate from each other. Obesity is one of the ways to do it; making trouble is another way.

GROVE   The good twin is the mother's favorite. She dotes over him. I'm not sure what to do with that.

HALEY   You know what I would think about doing? Besides bringing in grandmother when you can, I would bring the mother, the stepdad and the twins together and say that you're realizing they have a special problem because they have twins to deal with. This makes them not like other families. Twins are a special problem for parents and they're a special problem for each other. Because they're so much alike, they have the problem of being different from each other and of finding ways of being different from each other. For parents it's also very difficult to deal with twins. Because they're the same age, you can't put one in charge of the other like you can with an older child and a younger child. You don't have a way one can take care of the other. Start with something like that. Then say, "Now a man who comes in and marries a woman with twins has a special problem, because it's not the same as a family with two brothers." You make it a normal situation, but very, very special.

GROVE It's making the problem a two-person problem rather than one twin going bad.

HALEY Right. Say the "troublemaker" has had too much of a burden being the problem twin, and that his brother should replace him for one week.[1] Have the good twin say what he'd have to do to replace his brother for a week. He'd have to make some trouble at school. He'd have to throw his weight around and threaten people. He'd have to refuse to obey his mother and stepdad. Go through a list of depredations. Even if they don't do it, it will make it easier on the bad twin because you're not defining the problem as being in his nature. You're making it a problem of being twins.

GROVE It's shifting the framework of how they're thinking about the problem.

HALEY The stepfather further complicates this. You could say every stepfamily has a problem of how to integrate a stepfather into the family. Say, "The man comes into the family and the wife feels she needs his help, but at the same time she feels that he doesn't really know these boys. So when he starts to discipline the boys she feels he doesn't really understand them." I would start with a speech like that.

GROVE Give them a speech about stepfamilies.

HALEY I would start by seeing the mother alone and telling her

this. With this family together I think it would help to emphasize, "You've got a special problem that other families don't
have."

GROVE   I told the mother alone that she needs the stepdad's help.
She was hiding all of the boy's problems from her husband
because she feared he would get violent. I told her she just
needed an agreement with him that he would not use physical
punishment. That seemed to help.

HALEY   I would absolutely say that she has to let him do the dis-
ciplining his own way, with the one provision that there's no
violence. Anything else goes.

GROVE   That's your standard thing?

HALEY   Yes.

GROVE   I'm worried this boy may be interested in his biological
dad. He feels a loyalty to him and is rejecting the stepdad because of that.

HALEY   These boys haven't been with that man since they were
two. Generally, if you integrate the stepfather into the family,
so that he is behaving like the father, then the biological father
will show up and sometimes make trouble. I've seen them
show up even when you don't know how they found out what
the stepfather was doing.

GROVE   If I put the stepfather in charge, I should expect the father
to show up?

HALEY   Right. Then you get the father to agree that the stepfather
is the functioning father and the father can be like an uncle.
He can enjoy the kids if he wants to keep involved with them,
but he is not in the home every day to discipline the kids. He
has to let the stepfather do that.

GROVE   That's how you present it to the dad? He's not there every
day so he has to take a back seat. Aren't there some dads who
are resentful when you say that?

HALEY   Sure. You say, "You have to handle this because your kids will have nothing but trouble unless they can solve this problem of having two fathers." It's best for the boys if one father takes precedence. You ask the father, "Would you like to be called every day when all the problems come up? Do you think you can function as a father when you're not living with your kids?"

GROVE Have you had to give that speech?

HALEY I've said, "I don't see how you can do it."

GROVE Do you have these sessions with everybody together, or do you see them alone?

HALEY I'd see the biological father alone for that discussion. Just like I'd see the mother alone and say, "I know you're scared he (the stepdad) is going to harm these kids because he doesn't know them like you do, but you married him to get some help, so give him some room. Let him do it his own way." If you try to say that to the mother in front of the stepfather, the mother will usually say, "You want HIM in charge? He's the one who is doing such and such." You'll end up with an argument. If you see her alone and say that, she can usually accept it more easily.

GROVE The mother will take that suggestion in a different way if I give it to her individually. Do you think it's helpful to the kids if you have the two dads in together and have them state to the kids who is going to be the primary caretaker?

HALEY If you think one dad is provoking the kids to misbehave against the other dad, then absolutely bring them together.

GROVE With these twins, I think this biological dad is provoking the kids. I think he's jealous of the stepfather being married to his ex-wife.

HALEY If you think that, then I would have a session with the mother, the biological father, and the two kids and try to resolve this among the adults. To do that there's a strategy you can try. You use the question of the *kids'* adjustment to the parents' divorce as a reason to bring up the issues in front of all of the adults. Say to the parents that you think the kids have not accepted the divorce and that part of the reason the kids are making trouble is to try to get the parents back together. Then, to help the kids, you ask both parents to tell the kids that they are never going to get back together. Even if the mother got a divorce from her present husband, she would not go back with the father. Then ask the father to say that even if the mother would be single again, he would not want back with her again. If the father really does want back with her, he might then say, "Well, we might get back together some day." Then the mother has to say, "We're not going to ever get back together, I'm remarried now." You force the adults to clarify their positions in front of the kids.

GROVE You force the issue in front of the kids. What if the parents really are ambivalent about getting back together, and they say that in front of the kids?

HALEY Then you have to say that if the parents ever did get back together, it would not be based on anything the kids did or didn't do. If the kids were very good, or very bad, that would not influence the parents' decision.

GROVE OK.

HALEY What I would do for these two boys is to say to them, "You know, whoever runs the household and disciplines the children is the father, even if he isn't the man who provided the sperm and helped to conceive you." Tell the boys that starting now, you would like them to call their stepfather "dad." That might be very hard for them to do in the room. You can say, "It's not necessary, but it would be nice."

GROVE What are you going for here?

HALEY To raise the status of the stepfather, because "dad" is the man who is at home functioning as a father.

GROVE You say getting that started will often bring the biological father into the picture?

HALEY Getting the biological father into the picture often occurs when you get the mother to let the stepfather discipline the kids, and the kids begin to accept him and even call him dad. At that point, the biological father shows up. You'd be surprised how often I've seen that happen, and it wasn't because the therapist was looking for him.

GROVE   The father of these twins is in and out of the picture. Apparently the last time he showed up he threatened to beat up the stepfather because of jealousy over his ex-wife.

HALEY   That problem twin could be modeling himself on his dad. He's his father's son, he's not like his mother.

GROVE   If I ask the problem twin to call his stepfather "dad," he's going to say, "He's not my dad."

HALEY   Then you give a talk about what is a dad: "A dad is a man in the home who is married to your mother. A dad is the man of the house who has responsibility for you as a parent. A dad provides money for the family. Now the man who helped to produce you is your biological father. He's not your dad, though, because he's not living in the house. If he were living in the house, then he'd be your dad." I would give a talk like that.

GROVE   What do you do if you have a child who wants to be connected to the biological dad?

HALEY   If there is visitation, you have to say, "You've got two fathers and most kids don't have two fathers. They don't have two birthday presents, or two Christmas presents from two different fathers." You make it so they benefit from having two fathers. "You've got your biological father who you're going to see once a month, and you've got your dad at home." The biological father is "father." The functioning father is "dad."

GROVE   The issue is how to help the stepfather become more integrated into the household.

HALEY   Right. At this point he's treated like an outsider who is just living in the household. The problem for this stepfather is that these two boys are hers, and she will say to him "You don't really understand them." The man feels like an outsider in his own home.

With this stepfather, there's another thing you can do. Parents tend to divide kids. One takes one, and the other takes another. It looks like in this family mother has the good twin and stepfather has the hard one.

GROVE   That's exactly right.

HALEY   Sometimes you can say it isn't fair that father has to have the hard one, and suggest to them that they switch, and have mother take the hard one, and have father in charge of the easy one.

GROVE   When you say switching, I'm a little worried that the mother cannot handle the problem twin physically. He intimidates her.

HALEY   I suspect that she doesn't handle him because she wants the stepfather involved. He steps in to help her in those situations. You have to make it that if she has the hard one she has to handle him herself.

GROVE   No matter what? The stepfather says that when the boy is making trouble, the mother ineptly deals with him until the stepfather has to step in. I think the stepfather is the one who is most upset about the boy, so it would be very hard for him to resist coming in.

HALEY   He'd have to restrain himself and the mother would have to give him a signal that the boy is out of control.

GROVE   That's a nice idea.

HALEY   With a stepfather the goal is to have him either as a kindly figure in the life of the kids or as one of the adults who is responsible for the children's behavior.

GROVE   How do you decide which way to go?

HALEY   You talk to the mother and the stepfather, and ask, "Which do you want? How would you like it to turn out five years from now?"

GROVE   Do you ever talk to the kids about what they want?

HALEY   I don't think so. You're putting too much burden on them.

GROVE   How about their biological father?

HALEY   You can talk to the kids about how they want to relate to him, and then try to arrange that for them. With this family, he sounds like an unreliable character.

GROVE   He is. I'll be really curious to see if he shows up if I get this stepfather more integrated.

HALEY   If he does show up, one approach is to try to make him feel guilty about losing sight of what is best for the boys. You can say to him, "What you want is whatever is best for the boys. If you interfere with that, that would be a real shame. The kids would pay for it. So, let's talk about what role you could have that would be best for them."

Follow-Up

I followed through with several of these suggestions. All of the interventions seemed helpful; however, one in particular had a very profound impact. First, I had a school conference with the parents and various school personnel. It turned out that the school and parents were not communicating at all about the problems, and a few simple agreements between home and school put a stop to several of the "troublemaker" twin's problems there. With the family, I did give the talk about the special problem twins present, and I went on to frame the problem as one twin always having to be the "troublemaker." The "bad" twin loved this talk, and of course the "good" twin was not excited about taking his turn at being bad for a week. This little speech did seem to help. I also had the parents switch who was in charge of whom. The mother took over the problem twin, and the stepfather took over the with the "good" twin.

This took away the function of the problem twin's misbehavior. If he made trouble, it was an ordeal for the mother, rather than a way to keep the stepfather in the family.

By far the most profound intervention concerned what role the stepfather would have with the boys. I met with the mother alone and asked her what role she wanted her husband to have in the boys' life. The mother said she wanted him to be a father for them. I said to the mother that she would then have to allow her husband to handle the boys in his own way. This meant he could discipline them whatever way he saw fit, except violence. She agreed that this was reasonable. Next, I had the mother present this to her husband, and we all then met with the two boys. With everyone present I gave the speech about "What is a father?" As I spoke, the man sat more and more upright in his chair, and his wife looked at him with pride.

I concluded my speech by saying that the boys' stepdad fit the description in every way but there was one very important thing missing. The boys did not call him "dad." I therefore asked the boys if they could call him "dad" in the session. Both boys blushed, squirmed, and struggled with this. It was difficult to not insist they do it but still arrange for them to do it. The "good" twin did call the man "dad" after several agonizing minutes. The "bad" twin said he would like to call him "dad" but could not say it in the session. Later that week the mother called me up to tell me that the "bad" twin had indeed begun calling his stepfather "dad." As I was doing this intervention, the mood in the room made it obvious that it was exactly what had to be done. It had a very powerful impact on the whole group and the stepfather's status in the family was very clearly elevated.

Therapy ended with this family soon after this session. The "bad" twin shaped up at school, there was no more violence at home, and the mother was no longer depressed about the "whole family situation." No intervention was made directly with the biological father. I am uncertain how he responded to the boys' calling their stepfather "dad." One problem which was not adequately addressed in the therapy was the "bad" twin's weight problem. He continued to be fat. A follow-up call two months later found the boy to be doing fine in school and the mother to be in good spirits.

Discussion

Both blended families and therapists of blended families continue to struggle with how to integrate stepparents and stepfamilies in a way that both the adults and children can accept. In this approach, the problem is viewed hierarchically. We assume two primary issues have to be worked out: (1) what the role of the stepparent will be in the child's life, and (2) what the status of the noncustodial parent and stepparent will be in the child's life. One emotional challenge for everyone in blended families is the adjustment to a change in status of the adults in relation to the children.

From a hierarchical point of view, the day-to-day reality of living in a blended family can pose several paradoxes to both adults and children. The day-to-day reality puts the stepparent in a position of raising the children. This can be a serious problem if the stepparent does not have the status among the adults and the children in the family which is consistent with this reality. Likewise, the day-to-day reality of a noncustodial parent is that he is no longer able to function as a primary caretaker for the children. If this loss of status and role is denied, then again a paradox is imposed on the family. For example, if a noncustodial parent is involved in the daily problems of the children, such as getting them to do their homework or to take their baths, an organization inconsistent with the day-to-day reality of the family evolves, and problems can be anticipated.

We are not recommending that in every stepfamily the children be encouraged to call the stepparent "dad" or "mom." We are, however, assuming that the therapeutic challenge with blended families is primarily to help them find a way to structure their family that is consistent with the reality in which they find themselves. We also assume that if all of the adults, including both biological parents and stepparents, can create a plan which they can all live with and which accepts the realities of the situation, the children will spontaneously adjust and accept the various roles the adults are playing in their lives.

A FATHER WITH NO STATUS

This is a case of a 15-year-old boy who was referred for therapy after it was discovered that he was sexually abusing his 11-year-old sister. The boy was also chronically in trouble with the juvenile court system. He and his sister lived with their natural parents, who were on welfare.

The sex abuse was discovered by the mother during a time when the boy had run away from home. While he was out of the house, the daughter summoned the courage to tell her mother that the brother was sexually abusing her. The mother struggled to get the daughter to tell her all that had happened because the girl was feeling guilty that the boy had run away. She thought her brother had run away because he felt bad about the sex. The brother had been sexually fondling his sister and had had intercourse with her on several occasions. The fondling had been going on for at least two years. The girl did not feel right about it, but went along because the brother told her that, if she refused him, he would tell the parents and they both would get in trouble. On several occasions, the girl did refuse the brother, and he then forced himself on her.

The mother reported the girl's story to protective services. When the brother was located, he was evaluated for treatment, and it was recommended that he receive outpatient therapy for his sex abusing. He was sent home, and to protect the daughter from her brother, the family put a lock on her bedroom door. The family was then referred to our clinic with the understanding that if the brother did not cooperate with treatment, protective services would remove him from the home. I supervised the case from behind the mirror.

In the first session, we had the entire family come. The boy was denying to both protective services and to his parents the full extent of what he had done to his sister. In this session, however, in the presence of his family, we got the boy to confess everything he had done. We had him apologize on his knees to both of his parents, and his sister. The family felt very good about the boy's apology, and this session was especially helpful to the daughter.[2]

After this first session, several additional family problems became evident. The mother was very powerful in this family, and the father was totally inconsequential. The father was a man in his mid-forties who had been married once before. He looked much older than his age and usually came to the sessions dressed like he was trying to look like Elvis Presley. He would wear black shirts unbuttoned down to the middle of his chest, with his hair slicked back and his shirt collar turned up. In one session, referring to her husband and her son, the mother said, "I'm raising both of them." The couple was deeply divided. The most intense relationship in the family was between the mother and the son. For example, for years the mother and son would get into playful wrestling matches, with the father disapproving but unable to assert himself. There was a sexual quality to the mother-son relationship. This mother-son intensity also had a destructive side. The mother and son would get into intense arguments, which would escalate and end violently, with the boy destroying household items. At times, these arguments would end with the boy running away from home and staying away for days.

We were trying to intervene in this dyad, but with little success. At the time of this consultation the boy had recently run away again and had been picked up by the authorities. He was being held temporarily in a detention center. While in detention the boy said repeatedly that he did not want to return to his parents and would run away again if forced to go home. The parents were uncertain if they wanted him back or if they wanted him in a residential treatment facility. Besides myself and the therapist, protective services and a court worker were involved with the family. The professionals were divided about how to respond to the boy's most recent runaway.

HALEY   Where does he go when he runs away?

GROVE   He got with a gang and he has friends that will put him up. His parents are afraid of these friends. While he was gone, the boy kept a very close eye on the house. When the parents were out, he went in and got shampoo, and toothpaste, and things like that. Then he left again. I've got two problems here. One is getting him back home. Two is, if I do get him back there, how to organize this family so that the fighting between him and his mother stops and he stops running away.

HALEY   The sex with the sister has stopped?

GROVE   The sex with the sister has stopped. We put all our emphasis on whether she's afraid of him or not. That lock should come off the door when she's no longer afraid of him. She's to a point where she is not afraid of him sexually, but she's afraid of his tantrums. She's afraid that he'll have a temper tantrum and hurt her. The parents, on the other hand, equate his violence with the sexual exploitation of the girl. They say, "He can't control his urges. He can't control his urge to be violent; therefore, he can't control his sexual urges." Whenever he's violent, they say, "He still must have a sexual problem, too. He might go after her again." That's the parents' position. The girl isn't worried about him going after her sexually at all, at this point.

HALEY   She should know, I suspect.

GROVE   Right. I figured she would know if he's looking at her in a funny way, or saying anything to her. We put all the emphasis on how she feels about him.

HALEY   But what if he did try to break the lock? Who would save her?

GROVE   The mother would beat the crap out of that boy.

HALEY   The mother?

GROVE   Oh my God!

HALEY   The father wouldn't?

GROVE   The father is this soft-spoken man who says something idiotic when he does say something. When we did that first session and asked the father why the sex abuse was wrong, his response was, "Well, he could have gotten her pregnant and then that baby could be deformed!" That was his only reason why it was wrong. He and the son have had conversations about women like, "Look at the ass on that one!" My general problem is how to elevate this man.

HALEY Your problem is how to get him to intervene between the mother and the boy.

GROVE My first way was trying to set it up between mother and son and that didn't work. The intensity is too great for them to get away from each other. I struggle with these violent kids that run away. How to get the parents to take charge of that. I don't have a lot of good ideas on that general situation.

HALEY Is the father able to whip him?

GROVE I don't know. The mother would. The father has physical problems and says, "I can't take too much of this."

HALEY That's a problem. The professionals are all going to meet and decide?

GROVE Yes.

HALEY If the boy doesn't go home, where will the professionals put him?

GROVE I don't know. They have a serious problem. They have him in an unsecure detention facility now. He could run from there any day. He's telling them, "If you don't do what I want, I'm going to run away from here." He has all the power and he's using it, not only with the parents, but with the professionals. The protective service people are all calling me saying, "What should we do, because he could run away this weekend!"

HALEY The thing about running away is that it isn't so nice out there, particularly with winter coming on.

GROVE He does have places where he can stay though.

HALEY But, these are people's homes, right?

GROVE Yes.

HALEY   Are his parents up to telephoning those people and saying
it's illegal for him to stay there?

GROVE   I think we could get that if we knew the people he stays
with but, the boy isn't going to tell us that. He lives in a rough
area. When he's out, he's out running around with kids of ages
ranging from 15 to 20, kids in gangs. But also, there's another
problem here. There's a threat of separation with this couple.
The mother says, "If the boy's problem isn't solved, my husband and I will have to separate. The boy will have to go with
his dad. I'll take the girl." It makes me think that there was
some threat of separation between the two parents and the
boy responded by running away. There's no husband and wife
here at all. One question I've been asking myself is this: Is this
a boy who cares more about himself and gratifying his own
needs and wanting to leave and do his own thing, or is this a
boy who is responding to the threat of separation and is caught
up in that?

HALEY   You could have either hypothesis. I would prefer the latter.
The professionals all deal with mother?

GROVE   Yes.

HALEY   Is the mother at all involved with him sexually?

GROVE   There's a sexual quality to their relationship, but I don't
know of any actual sexual incidents.
      If he were back home, we could put the father more in
charge of the boy. We could tell the mother that he's at an age
now where she has to change her relationship with him, because of his sexual problems.

HALEY   I would definitely do that, but I would say because he's 15.

GROVE   Because he's 15. But also, I think we should make it sexual.
There won't be any more wrestling matches between the boy
and his mother if she thinks he might be thinking of that as a
sexual encounter. But if I do put the father in charge, I'm not
sure what to do with him. What would you do with this inept
man? How would you get him involved with this boy? There

are two problems. One is getting the father to do something reasonable and two is getting the mother to allow the father to be in charge in the first place.

HALEY   I would give him custody.

GROVE   Explain that.

HALEY   If the professionals as a group would all say, "Father has to be in charge of this boy. He's now out of puberty and a man." Then the professionals only deal with father.

GROVE   Father brings him to therapy without mother?

HALEY   That can happen. Or father deals with the community, and goes to the court, and mother stays home.

GROVE   I suppose we could do that. But the mother's going to say, "My husband doesn't know what to do because I have to raise him too. The things he does are crazy."

HALEY   They probably are; that's the problem. You could hint at how this might affect the boy's sexual development.

GROVE   Say more about that.

HALEY   If she were scared that, if the father doesn't take charge more, her son might turn out to be abnormal sexually, she might let him take over the boy. Most mothers are worried about their son's sexual orientation. If she thought that, I think she'd see to it that father took charge more.

GROVE   Yes. We could say something like, "This is a very critical time for his sexual development."

HALEY   Yes.

GROVE   But if we don't have that, what else could we say?

HALEY   Well, if the father is really inadequate you have a problem. If he's just being inadequate so his wife will do it, then you can essentially force him to take charge of the boy. But the first thing I would do is not assume that running away is a happy time for that boy, particularly if he's coming home to get a toothbrush. He doesn't have anything! He hasn't got any money out there!

GROVE   You're right, he got picked up for shoplifting.

HALEY   Trying to get something to eat probably! I think he may be out with his friends, but then they all go home. Where does he go? He has to go with one of them. Then he's an intruder, and temporary.

GROVE   He has to make that arrangement every night. But he doesn't present it as a hardship, obviously. He has everybody fooled, including me sometimes.

HALEY   Sure. Thinking it's great out there.

GROVE   Would you just say to everybody, "I don't think it really is all that great for him"?

HALEY   Sure.

GROVE   One idea would be to get the kid alone and try and persuade him that home is the best place. He's saying that counseling isn't helping, "Mom isn't changing at all. She's not doing what she's supposed to do." I might be able to get him to drop his runaway threat, if the mother really would let dad be in charge.

That's the angle! I think we'd have more chance of persuading the mother to back off if we make it a sacrifice she could make in the interest of seeing if her son would come home over that.

HALEY   If the boy will stop running away, or threatening to run away.

GROVE   Right. If we did that, do you think that would be insulting to her?

HALEY   I don't think so. I think you should say that by running away he's asserting his manhood.

GROVE   "Asserting his manhood." That's very good. That could be the general framework for the whole therapy. How to get him to assert his manhood in a proper way that isn't going to get him in trouble.

HALEY   Without being like the father, as far as the mother is concerned. She must be spurring this boy on to have some spirit and assert himself so he won't be like his father.

GROVE   Right. But if she doesn't want him to be like the father, then wouldn't putting the father in charge be a problem?

HALEY   You could tell her that if the father's in charge, her son will learn to be better than the father. You have to persuade her of that. He'll learn from the father not to be like the father. He'll rebel and be different.

GROVE   Essentially what we're doing here is asking the mother to let us help her to get her husband to be a competent dad, instead of her having to help the boy all by herself.

HALEY   Sure.

GROVE   I think that would be a major challenge for this woman. What we're asking her to do is to take a back seat. This is a lady who has been in complete charge of this family for a long time.

HALEY   Sure.

GROVE   I know what she can do! She could concentrate on helping the daughter.

HALEY   That's just what I was going to say. The daughter must have some problems.

GROVE   She does. She still has nightmares about the brother attacking her. She also feels different from the other girls because she was sexually abused. She thinks, "I was abused, and they weren't." She feels strange, and she worries that her teacher might ask her someday if this ever happened to her. Then because her mother has taught her never to lie, she'd have to tell them. But she doesn't want anyone to know she has been sexually abused.

HALEY   That's liable to happen in schools these days! They have discussions like that.

GROVE   That's true. The teachers are organizing discussions about sex abuse and she's worried that everyone's going to go around the room, and when it is her turn to talk she'll have to say what happened to her.

HALEY   The mother should find a way to solve that one, particularly. She could tell the daughter that when the teacher says, "Did it happen to you?" she's to say, "My mother told me not to talk about sex." Then the school would have to deal with the mother.

GROVE   Yes.

HALEY   What's the husband do for a living?

GROVE   He doesn't work. This is a welfare family.

HALEY   Oh, he's just out of it all over.

GROVE   Right.

HALEY   The problem is that so many women take charge in the home, and the husband works outside and takes charge outside. That is usually not a problem. But if the husband doesn't work outside the home, he often has a real problem in the home.

GROVE   He doesn't have a purpose.

HALEY   He has nothing. The welfare check goes to the woman. She then doles him out an allowance.

GROVE   Yes. I never thought of it that way. That's right.

HALEY   I used to think that if the government really wanted to make some changes among the poor they should give the welfare check to the men. Hopefully that would transform the irresponsible men and their families.

GROVE   I've had that exact same idea. Essentially there's no reason for the men to stay at home.

HALEY   If they can't work, they have to attach to a woman to get some money. You've got a classic problem there. As it is now, that father is not contributing anything to the family and therefore he has no purpose at home. His wife's in charge of the children and she brings in all of the money. One reason for putting a man like that in charge of helping his son is that he then has something he can do to contribute.

GROVE   Let's talk more about how to arrange for the boy to go back home. Here's the issue; there's going to be a court date now because the boy shoplifted. The parents also filed "unruly" charges on him.

HALEY   Could the court make father responsible for him?

GROVE   How do you mean? Do you mean legally?

HALEY   I'm still thinking about how to legally put the boy in custody of father.

GROVE   What's your thought?

HALEY   I just think that the father isn't strong enough to go against the mother all by himself. Therefore, he needs a coalition with somebody outside the family, like the court or the professionals, who will say he has to do this. Then he can say to his wife, "Well, they say I have to."

GROVE   Yes.

HALEY   The court can put him in charge. Without that, the mother's just going to take charge.

GROVE   But I think we can put him in charge.

HALEY   If you do it, then I think you first have to clear it with the mother and get her permission. I think you have to go through power, or go to power. The mother has power, and the boy has power. I would also accept the boy's power.

GROVE   Ask the boy what the rules should be if he goes back home?

HALEY   Put the boy in charge of his own behavior, with the parents' permission.

GROVE   Then have the father deal out the consequences, not the mother.

HALEY   The mother has to put the father in charge. That man is not going to go out and take it.

GROVE   Right.

HALEY   That's what Erickson used to say. He would persuade a mother that biologically a child needs a father, otherwise they won't be normal. No mother wants an abnormal child. Therefore, one duty of the mother has to be for her to see to it that her child experiences the influence of the father. When he put it to her that way, the mother would arrange for the father to have his influence. That's the way Erickson did it.

GROVE Well, this is a very complex case.

HALEY I don't think it's a simple thing. You have the classic family, of a father out of it all. The mother has the money. The mother is in charge of the boy. The boy is misbehaving. Probably to get father involved. You have to find a way to get father involved with mother allowing him. I think a teenage boy in that situation will escalate until the father takes charge.

GROVE I think that's exactly what's happening. Mother and son are an unstable dyad. When they fight, the father doesn't get involved, so the mother and son escalate to a point where they have to get away from each other on their own, or until outsiders come into it.

HALEY The mother assumes that if they split the boy would go with his father?

GROVE Yes.

HALEY I would see her alone if she has that idea. Say that just in the chance that might happen, she should see to it that father can handle that boy.

GROVE That sounds like that might work. Another issue is that protective services right now is calling the shots on who's going to do what treatment and they want a meeting with the parents in the room.

HALEY If there's a meeting with the professionals and the parents, it's appropriate to ask the parents what they think about the situation. I would ask the mother what she feels father should be doing to help straighten that boy out. Then later, you can nail her on her own words.

GROVE She'll say it too. She always says the right things.

HALEY I'm sure.

GROVE I think that's the best way to go. We can say everything you and I have talked about. We can say that emotionally the boy needs the guidance of a father. That can be said in the presence of the professionals.

HALEY I would also say to the professionals that the boy doesn't have it that good out on the street. That's a power ploy, really. To say, "Boy, I've got it made out there." Then the parents say, "Oh, please stay with us."

GROVE You're saying it's hot air. I think you're right, the boy really wants to go home. He just wants a different circumstance to go home to. If we can arrange that, he'll go back and settle down.

HALEY If he's in somebody else's house, what about school? Does he go off to school from there? Does he stay home? If he stays home, are the parents in that house objecting to him being around the house all the time? Does he have to stay outside the house? Not everybody lets a problem kid come stay in their house and hang out there all day.

After this consultation, the therapist and I met and made a plan for putting the father in charge of the boy. This would be the main strategy of the case. Accomplishing this took several steps. We first met with the mother alone. We put our emphasis on helping the boy learn how to assert his manhood in a way that does not involve violence or sexual offenses on women. We explained that for the boy to accomplish this at the age he is now, he would need the influence of his father, and that we would guide her husband regarding what he needs to do to help. We also explained that we continued to worry about the problems her daughter was expressing about the sexual abuse and that we thought she (the mother) could concentrate more on helping her daughter if she did not have to be so preoccupied with her son. The mother was very agreeable to this. We then met with the mother and father, and we had the mother explain to her husband that from now on he would be in charge of the son and that the therapist would help him determine what to do. The father was nervous about having this responsibility, but he agreed to try it. With the parents' permission, we next met with the boy alone. We asked him what rules he would want regarding his behavior for him to be willing to return home. He came up with very reasonable expectations for himself. We then met with the whole family. With everyone present, we had the mother explain to her son that his father would be in charge of him. We had the boy propose to his father the rules which the boy had laid out. This got the family past the impasse of whether or not the boy would willingly go home. He went home the day after this session.

We worked with this plan for the next two months. The mother did an excellent job of helping the daughter. She and the daughter had some very nice mother-daughter talks, and the daughter was clearly becoming less upset about the sex abuse. The father, on the other hand, struggled with the son. Despite these interventions, the mother and son were still having violent exchanges at home, and the mother continued to express concern that the boy was not really over his sexual problems.

Two Months Later

GROVE   I did a little field experiment with this family. When the boy finally had his court date, the therapist and I joined the family at court. While we were all waiting out in the hall to go in front of the judge, I was watching how the family members were acting with each other. What I saw was incredible. The mother and son were standing facing each other, with their faces about three inches apart. They were standing there talking and laughing with each other. If you didn't know them you would think they were boyfriend and girlfriend! While this was going on, the father was helplessly off to the side, obviously disapproving. When I saw this I thought, "All right, I'm going to go and try something."

I decided to see what would happen if the parents could

warm up to each other. I went over and casually struck up a conversation with the father about how he and the mother first met. The mother came over, and the two of them started to tell an incredible story of how when they first met the husband had a prestigious factory job and a big convertible. The father swept the mother off her feet, driving her around in his big convertible. The mother was talking with a big smile on her face and the father was standing there bragging. They were both obviously enjoying it. Now, listen to this. The boy allowed this talk to go on for about one minute! He came over and started berating his father. He said, "Did you remember to put your teeth in today, dad? You really look like Elvis today, dad." Within about thirty seconds he not only broke up this nice conversation, but he also had his dad close to tears.

HALEY   Isn't that something!

GROVE   Let me tell you what else I found out and then I'll tell you what I'm confused about. When the couple were first married, the man had this very good factory job. He was making a lot of money and had a lot of status in his family. He had extended family who would come to him for financial help. He was the most powerful man in his family. Then after several years, he developed the famous mystery back pain. He lost his job and all of his status. Now the man has nothing. This is what confuses me. When the boy ran away last, it was right after the mother threatened to leave the father. I was thinking the boy's symptoms are keeping the couple together. Then I see what happened at court. The boy won't even let them have a nice conversation! I'm confused about this boy's motivation.

HALEY   It sounds like he regulates their distance. I would assume that man's back pain is his way of managing his wife. They might have fought over his work, or they had some issue between them that his back pain relates to. I would also assume that they have some serious sexual problems.

GROVE   Explain that.

HALEY   The couple can't get distance and split, or the dad will probably fall apart. I'm sure the boy reacts to prevent that. But if they start warming up to each other and showing affection, that might lead to sex or raise the question of whether they will have sex. If having sex is a problem, the boy has to help them with that too.

GROVE   How do we solve this?

HALEY   You have to draw a boundary around that couple and get the boy out of that.

GROVE   Do you have ideas on that?

HALEY   One Erickson way would be to have the parents talk, in the presence of the boy, about when the boy was an infant. That is, you ask them in his presence what it was like raising him when he was little. What was his birth like? Did he cry a lot? Who changed his diapers? That talk will put him lower hierarchically in relation to them. It'll be hard for the mother and son to have a "sexy" relationship when the parents are talking about how much he pooped when he was a baby. Also, that's a time he doesn't even remember, when his parents were more together as a couple.

GROVE   I like that. We can do that. Do you think that alone will be strong enough though?

HALEY   Probably not.

GROVE   What else can we do?

HALEY   You could do an intervention Cloé has used.[3] You would have to find an excuse to ask the parents to do this. You could tell the parents alone, "One thing that is very important for your son to learn is how to treat women with affection. The best way he can learn this is from you two." Then set it up, so they start hugging and kissing in front of the boy, when the boy doesn't expect it.

GROVE   Cloé uses that intervention with young couples to help the couple make a boundary with intrusive in-laws. You're saying to use that here to draw a boundary between the parents and the son.

HALEY That's right. That boy would be so confused if he saw them doing that. He wouldn't know what to do probably.

GROVE That's right, he wouldn't.

HALEY You could tell the parents this is important for the boy's education, so even if they are upset with each other, maybe they could pretend to be affectionate when their son's around.

GROVE There's another thing that's good about that. It's another way for the father to intervene between his wife and his son. The mother's relationship with her son has definite sexual overtones. What I finally realized is that she violated a boundary with her son, and he then violated a boundary with his sister. That probably happened after the husband and wife stopped having sex.

HALEY I would still worry about that boy going after his sister again as long as the mother and father are so apart sexually.

Follow-Up

This case has a mixed outcome. My involvement with this family as supervisor of the therapist ended soon after the above consultation. I left the clinic and went into private practice. Six months later, however, I contacted the therapist, who was still working with the family, and the two of us had a lengthy discussion about how they were doing. I learned that the mother opened up at length to the therapist about her dissatisfactions with her husband. The therapist then became intensely involved with the couple around marital issues. I believe this freed the boy from his entanglement with his parents.

Both children had improved significantly. Neither the daughter nor the mother was afraid of the boy sexually abusing his sister again. The girl seemed totally free from any distress related to the sex abuse. She no longer was having nightmares, she no longer feared the possibility of her teacher discussing it with her, and she was showing no signs of continued distress. The boy had also improved greatly. The therapist continued working with the boy and the family around sex offender issues, which involved reparation for the victim, sex education for the boy, and helping the boy have more empathy for his sister. The boy responded by improving at school, finding a nice girlfriend his own age, and avoiding violence both at home and at school. He has not run away from home and there have been no further juvenile charges filed against him.

The therapist's attempts at improving the couple's marriage, however, have thus far failed. The husband continues to be very down in relation to his wife. Although the therapist has succeeded at getting the son out of a triangle with his parents, she has not succeeded at getting herself out of a triangle with them. I told her that I thought she would be stuck with them until she managed to raise the husband's status in relation to his wife.

Discussion

GROVE I wanted to ask you something about "putting fathers in charge." I have so many cases where it's just clear that if the father would step in and do something the problem would be solved. At one point you were talking to the trainees, giving a little history of family therapy ideas, saying that you went awhile putting the peripheral fathers in charge, and you realized that that produced marital conflict. At one point you thought the marital conflict was just a stage of the therapy. Then you went to putting the involved mothers in charge, and getting them to help the child over the problems without father stepping in. That procedure did not produce a marital conflict stage, so you were encouraging therapists to experiment with that route. But now it seems to me that on these cases you and I are discussing we're back to putting the father in charge again. Is there some difference in these cases? Has your thinking changed on this again? What's going on here?

HALEY I still think you often don't get a marital conflict stage if you put the mother in charge. But you apparently also don't resolve any issues between mother and father that are a problem.

GROVE In some situations if you help the mother solve it by herself, there will still be something left unfinished.

HALEY Sure. I just think it's a matter of a dual hierarchy. So often, the men are in charge outside the home, and the women are in charge in the home. When a woman is in charge of the children in the home, and you take the father and put him in charge, you're disrupting a basic hierarchical situation. They are going to have conflict. Often the husband has avoided conflicts with his wife about the children, like who's going to take charge, who's going to make them study, and so on.

GROVE Let me tell you what happened with a family I'm working with. This is a family with a teenage son who is a drug addict and has repeatedly run away from home. The mother has always protected the boy. She finds out when he's in trouble and keeps it a secret from her husband. Then finally she can't keep what the boy's doing a secret from her husband any longer and the husband blows up and throws the boy out of the house. I started by putting the mother in charge of dealing with the boy on her own and asking the father to take a vacation. She then arranged on her own for the father to be in charge. I worked with the mother to take charge of this boy and she struggled with that. The more I worked with her, the more I realized it was an error for me to have the mother in charge. The mother seemed to have the agenda for her husband to solve the boy's problem. She was concerned about the relationship between her husband and son and her stepping in and solving the problem would not change the father-son relationship. I then had to figure out how to put the father in charge after I started out the way I did. I finally worked it out for the father to take charge and he stepped in and did something positive with the boy.

The mother was so pleased that her husband and son got together. It became obvious that all along she had an agenda to get her husband to do something helpful with the son. When he finally did, she was so pleased. Now, that makes me think that no amount of getting the mother to do anything would have solved that problem. You see what I mean? She was only going to be satisfied when her husband did something helpful.

HALEY There seem to be times when that becomes so evident. Kids will have a symptom, and they'll escalate it, and mother will try to deal with it, and mother and son will keep escalating until father gets involved.

GROVE Right. I've got six cases like that.

HALEY When that seems to be the whole function of the escalation, you just about have to put the father in charge.

• • • • • • •

HALEY One traditional problem triangle is a father, teenage daughter, jealous mother triangle. In that situation you usually have a father and his teenage daughter in too close of a relationship with each other, and the mother jealous. One symptom of that triangle is a jealous type of fighting between mother and daughter. Some mothers have a real problem with the idea that they're fading as their daughters are blossoming. The father's caught right in the middle. The daughter discovers that father can enjoy her company more than he does mother's. At that point, the daughter may get flirtatious with him. If that happens, the mother's going to begin to get into it with the daughter. But they're not going to fight openly over the father's attention. They're going to fight about something else.

GROVE What have you done with those?

HALEY You try to look for some simple intervention. One intervention you can try occasionally, if you think it's appropriate, is to have the father take the daughter out to lunch. You frame it to the family that, as the daughter is becoming interested in boys, or has a boyfriend, it would be helpful for her to have the opportunity to go out with a nice man to a nice place. Then she'll have a positive experience with which she can compare her future dealings with boyfriends. You can involve the mother in this by having her help the daughter pick out a nice dress to wear and to help her look her best. Then father takes her to a nice restaurant.

GROVE   You're creating the situation the mother's jealous about.

HALEY   Right. What you might think would happen with this is that, if a father takes his daughter out to lunch, they might then get even closer together. But what actually happens is they get farther apart. When people look at them in the restaurant, they suspect they might be mistaken for an older man with a young girlfriend.

GROVE   You're saying that if you have a father and daughter who are too close, rather than trying to pry them apart, you push them closer together. They then respond by moving apart spontaneously.

HALEY   Right. What also usually happens is that the husband will then get closer to his wife.

GROVE   So the trick is to put some repellent there between the daughter and the father.

HALEY   That's right.

GROVE   The father will then go back toward his wife. The wife can then be happy that he's done that and the mother and daughter will stop fighting.

HALEY   If you try to solve that jealousy by offering an interpretation that something like that is going on, the father and daughter won't want anyone thinking they're too close, so they might get covertly close and that would raise even more suspicion.

GROVE   If you just announced that the father and daughter were too close, that would also not necessarily result in the husband spontaneously moving toward his wife. If he did move towards

his wife, it would be because a therapist made the announcement that he and the daughter were too close, not because
he was doing it on his own. The wife may not receive his
advances.

HALEY   That's right. An interpretation makes everybody uncomfortable with the whole situation, whereas, if you push father
and daughter to be closer, they'll respond by getting distant.
You assume they can't tolerate the closeness you're asking for.
It's interesting that I've had a father take his daughter out to
lunch, and they laugh about it afterwards, but it wasn't so
funny the way people looked at them when they were out
together.

GROVE   The daughter makes herself pretty and everybody wonders,
"Is this an older man taking out a younger woman?" They get
uncomfortable and say, "Oh, my God we don't want anyone
getting the wrong idea!"

HALEY   That's right. You make them act out explicitly what the
family is implicitly fighting about.

GROVE   It's made explicit by your task.

2 | MARITAL CONTRACTS

WE SOMETIMES ASSUME a symptom presented by a spouse in therapy expresses a marital contract; that is, the symptom is viewed as having a stabilizing function in the couple's marriage.[1] In some cases a client will overcome a symptom working individually in therapy and the spouse will adjust to the change with no problem. In other cases, however, no matter how innovative the intervention offered by a therapist, if the spouse is left out of the therapist's office or of the therapist's thinking, the therapy will fail. The client's spouse will be unable to accommodate to the changes produced by the therapy. If the client is seen individually, the therapy may reach an impasse, or the client may improve and then relapse. One explanation for this is that, by excluding the client's spouse, the therapy is stabilizing the couple in their current arrangement.

These situations suggest that it is generally a good idea to involve the client's spouse in whatever therapy is offered. Whatever the framework of the therapy, or the style of the therapist, if the spouse is involved, he or she is more likely to accommodate to the changes produced by the therapy. Conceptualizing symptoms presented by a spouse as having a stabilizing function in a couple's marriage means simply that the client's spouse should be invited to participate in the solving of the problem. We assume that involving the client's spouse directly in the therapy is often the most efficient way to solve a problem when an individual symptom is presented as the difficulty.

When one spouse with an individual symptom seeks therapy, the goal in this approach is not only to eliminate the symptom being presented as the problem, but also to help the couple change the marriage so that it is not necessary for one of the spouses to have a symptom. Two issues are implicit. First, if a spouse comes to therapy with an individual symptom and the marriage is hypothesized to be the problem, we do not attempt to interpret the problem as a "bad marriage." For example, if a woman comes to therapy presenting herself as the one with a problem, we would generally consider it an error to try to convince her that she has a marital problem. We would assume that she wants help with her husband, but she understands that her husband is reluctant to have the problem described as the marriage. We would also assume that, if we were to attempt to impose this reframing on the woman, she would probably never bring her husband to therapy and we might even lose her. Out of respect for her, we would accept her way of describing the problem.

The second issue involves what we assume will be most helpful to a spouse in this situation. A woman may have a symptom and may also have serious complaints about her marriage. Her husband may have serious problems and the woman may be ambivalent about staying with him. Should the therapist encourage the couple to split? We would consider this a very serious error. We would assume that what the woman really wants is help from the therapist in getting her husband to improve himself. Often if the husband can improve himself, the wife happily stays with him. That is what the strategies we discuss are designed to accomplish.

A DEPRESSED AND ANXIOUS WIFE

This is a case of a 27-year-old woman who desperately sought therapy for two symptoms: depression and panic attacks. The young woman lived with her 44-year-old husband and their two little boys, ages three and five. The client came to the first interview in very bad shape. She was dressed in a ragged sweatsuit, wearing no makeup, and her hair was messy. She began the interview visibly shaking, and sweating. She explained that three months earlier she had spent six weeks in the hospital due to depression. She was now experiencing once again the same level of depression she had had just prior to being hospitalized. She was very afraid that if she did not improve soon, she would end up back in the hospital.

She was very open with me in this first interview. She gave a wealth of information describing a very complex family situation, as well as very traumatic past events. She explained that one incident in her life continued to disturb her. At age 13 she was sexually abused by an older stepbrother. At 17 she had her first boyfriend and confided in him about the abuse. The boyfriend became jealous of her brother and considered him a sexual rival. When she decided to break up with the boyfriend, he became totally irrational and shot and killed the woman's brother. The client explained that this event continued to weigh heavily on her.

In her present circumstances, she was very upset with her mother, who was living a carefree life. She was constantly getting herself into financial trouble and then looking to my client for help. She complained that her mother frequently imposed on her by asking her to drop whatever she might be doing and to come and rescue the mother from whatever trouble she was in. On the other hand, the mother never helped my client with anything.

She was also very upset about her marriage. Since her panic attacks occurred at night, I began to suspect that this problem was related to sex. She explained that after she and her husband were married he withdrew from her sexually. She was very upset about this and would pressure him for sex. He continued to refuse her. At one point he instructed her to find a boyfriend to satisfy her sexual needs. She did not want to do this, but to please him she began to date another man. The husband then became very jealous, so she broke up with the boyfriend. She then told me about a pattern for which I concluded her panic attacks became a metaphor. She would go to bed at night and want to have sex. Her husband would refuse her, and she would become very upset. He would then console her and comfort her to calm her down. In this first interview she explained that now when she goes to bed she begins to get anxious and panicky. Her husband then will console her and calm her down, just as he did before when she pressured him for sex. Now, however, the topic of having sex is no longer even mentioned. Instead, the client said she had just resigned herself to the idea that she and her husband would never have sex.

My problem in this interview was to assess which of these many problems was crucial to her acute depression. She explained that she had always been sad since the death of her brother ten years earlier. Her hospitalization, however, was due to an acute depression which began six months prior to the therapy. I asked her what she would be doing if she did not have her depression. She explained that she would be working, would lose weight, would complete her household responsibilities each day and would be saying "no" to her mother. I asked her who in the family would have the most difficult time adjusting if she made these changes. She said emphatically that her husband would have the hardest time.

Because she was so desperate, I knew I had to end the first session by giving her some directive aimed at reducing her depression. I explained that a first step would be for her to get control of her own emotions. One way to accomplish this would be to see if she could make herself depressed on purpose. I therefore asked her to schedule two hours of depression each day. She could get up, not take a shower, put on a ragged robe, and sit around thinking depressing thoughts for two hours per day. Then she could have the rest of the day to do what she wanted. I also insisted that she bring her husband the next time.

She did bring her husband to the next interview, and the two of them made a dramatic impression. She came in looking great. Her hair was done, she was wearing makeup and nice clothes, and she was visibly much less anxious. Her husband, on the other hand, had long scraggly hair and a scruffy beard. He was wearing blue jeans smeared with grease, with holes in both knees and in the buttocks. He sat slumped in his chair and had very little to say the whole interview. The wife explained that she had had no depression the whole week. She did not schedule her two hours of depression. Instead she joined Weight Watchers, did all her housework, and began looking for a job. I explained, emphatically, that if her depression returned, she owed me my two hours.

At this point, it was obvious that the husband was the problem. I tried to set up a strategy where the husband would help his wife with her recovery. My thought was that he could then be given credit for her improvement, and this would help to raise his self-esteem. The husband, however, did not cooperate with this. He would come to the sessions intermittently, and did not assert himself in any way to help his wife. The wife continued to improve dramatically, but I was very concerned that the therapy would fail if the husband stayed as he was.

GROVE   The wife is improving very rapidly. The husband is not doing anything. He's stuck in the mud. One big problem is that he is totally unhappy with his work. He hates his job, but he doesn't feel that he can do anything else. He and I came up with some ideas on what he might do about that, but he's not doing anything about it. I'm very worried that she is not going to be able to maintain her improvement if he stays stuck where he is.

At this point there is a constant pressure for her to relapse as long as the husband does not improve. She has now started a job. When she came home from her first day at the job, he complained to her about all the trouble that the children made while she was away. He doesn't want to have to watch them if they are going to be so much trouble. His complaining makes her uncomfortable about her improvement.

I got him alone and I talked to him about how helpful he'd been to her so far, and said that I thought that he should think about how bad things were when she went into the hospital.

They lost a lot of money because of her hospital bill, and when she was in the hospital he was stuck at home with the kids. Then when she came home she wasn't doing anything around the house. I told him that, if all it takes is for her to have a job and lose a little weight to prevent things from going back to how it was before, then it's worth it to him to help her. I don't think that speech helped much though. My problem is getting him to improve, now that she is doing so well.

HALEY   I think your hypothesis is correct that he is involved in her having her problems.

GROVE   I'm very worried that she's going to lose weight and he's going to be jealous and insecure. He's an older man who is neglecting her sexually. One of the big problems is that they have no sex. She has basically resigned herself to that as the way it's going to be. I think the sexual problems are part of why she gets anxiety attacks at night. She's taking medicine to control her anxiety. She says she's most concerned about her depression and she wants to make sure that that problem is gone before she works on the panic attacks. With the panic attacks she prefers to just take medicine. At this point I don't want to try and wrestle the medicine away from her.

HALEY   Apparently the agreement she and her husband have is that she's the patient.

GROVE   Yes, that's right.

HALEY   To keep the agreement going, she has to have some announcement that she's the patient. That's what the medication can do. If he doesn't take medicine, and she does, then she's the patient. I would agree with you that the anxiety at night is related to sex. She's in an impossible situation with her marriage, and that often goes with depression. She can't tolerate her life with her husband, and she can't leave him because of her children.

GROVE   That's right. It's clear that that's how it is. It's even more clear now that she's changing and he isn't.

HALEY She seems to be changing in relation to you. You provided some energy in her life by giving her things to do.

GROVE She's on a weight loss program, which is a social thing too, because it's Weight Watchers. She found a job. She looks much better. She always comes in now made up and looking nice. She's more cheerful. It makes me worry that if the husband stays the same, she will go right back downhill.

HALEY I would worry more about splitting them. If she cooperates and wants to improve, she's going to please you. He's going to find her pleased by another man. He's still "stuck in the mud" while she's changing, so she might leave him for that reason.

GROVE I think that's very possible. She's talked about splitting with him. When she was depressed she said, "I don't know if I can stay with him." I may have contributed to it already because I said, "Look, you should just get stronger, and improve, and once you're in a better state of mind you'll know better what you should do about that."

HALEY If he stays in the mud, as you say, she either has to relapse or leave. Those are the choices she's forced into, really.

GROVE Here's one of the dilemmas: I've thought about getting him alone and saying, "I'm worried you're going to lose her."

HALEY That's right.

GROVE But I'm hesitant to do that because how do you help a man with low self esteem? Do you get him alone and tell him, "You're going to lose your wife"? You think I should do that?

HALEY If she brings him in, and she is looking pretty good, I would see him alone and apologize to him.

GROVE I apologize to him!

HALEY Right. Say that you feel that you've been tampering with their marriage without really intending to. That your job was to help her over her depression, to make her have higher self-esteem and to feel better.

GROVE "Now, because of me, you have a different woman on

your hands. She's going to be more assertive, she's going to be stronger." I didn't think of apologizing to him.

HALEY   You can say your job was to help her with her individual problems and the therapy has had this effect on their marriage.

GROVE   Right. The effect on their marriage was not what I intended.

HALEY   I think you have a half a chance if you do it that way. He must have been trying to get her to improve in various ways over the years, and she didn't. She just got depressed with him. Then you come into the picture and she blossoms.

GROVE   Yes, it makes him look bad.

HALEY   If he is to join you in doing something about himself and his marriage, somehow you have to step down in relation to him.

GROVE   You're saying give him some room to maneuver by stepping down.

HALEY   Sure. I'd tell him that she's becoming more unpredictable in what she might do, and he could handle this by being more unpredictable himself. What can he do this week that would surprise her?

GROVE   Do you think I should tell him I'm worried he might lose her?

HALEY   I think so. He must know that anyway. You can say that she's growing and developing and so she's going to expect more out of him. He's going to have to deliver or he might lose her.

GROVE   Then apologize to him for that. "I'm sorry I've helped to create this."

HALEY   You can apologize because it's true. You helped to set up this situation.

GROVE   I see that.

HALEY   Generally, if you can, you start by having a husband help his unhappy wife. As he succeeds in helping her improve, he will start to feel better. I would assume that is what the wife wants. If you have a man who won't do that, then you have to start with the wife and you're into this dilemma.

GROVE Right, she's improving and he isn't.

HALEY She's improving because of another man.

GROVE Yes.

HALEY One problem is that he might try to defeat you if he's resentful of what you've done for his wife. If that's true, he'll end up not cooperating with you. That's the very thing that's going to cause him the most trouble with his wife. Your problem is going to be getting him started initiating things that aren't what you tell him to do.

GROVE Right, so it's not my advice. But what you're saying is, if I apologize and tell him that she's improving now so she's going to expect more out of him, that's still pretty general. That gives him enough room to maneuver. It gives him something to worry about, but then it also gives him some room to come up with something on his own.

HALEY Yes. I'm sure what he's worried about is she's becoming more unpredictable. She's losing weight, she's working, God knows what she'll do next! So you have to say that he has to do some unpredictable things in order to be together with her more. So what can he do this week that would surprise her? Like, what if he came home and said, "We're going out to dinner tonight, I've arranged for a sitter." She'd probably fall out of her chair. Or you can make a not very good suggestion, so that he can correct you and think of a better one on his own.

GROVE Set it up so he can reject my idea.

HALEY You can say, "You know your wife so well, certainly better than I know her, because I hardly know her." You have to get out of the relationship where you're superior to him in relation to his wife. Say, "You must know of things that would please her, or displease her . . . maybe you'd like to surprise her by displeasing her." So he has the whole range of something to think about. What does he do for a living?

GROVE   He's a custodian in an office building. He's been there many years and his boss mistreats him. It would be a big change for him to leave there.

HALEY   Would he lose a pension if he left?

GROVE   No. The company recently cut his benefits. Now he has to pay a lot more money for health insurance. That's been a major blow to him. I think that's when the wife took a downturn and became depressed. She wants him to get another job. He says he wants to, but he doesn't act like it.

HALEY   I would spend some time with him alone talking about changing careers and what sort of jobs he would be interested in. Have there been things in his life that he was tempted toward, but never did? Something to get him interested in thinking beyond the horizon of that job.

GROVE   What I really like about what you just said is the idea of getting him to think beyond the horizon about anything.

HALEY   (laughs) That's right.

GROVE   This man thinks of his life as over.

HALEY   I would normalize that by saying many people have problems when they reach their forties. Sometimes they don't like what they're doing, but they don't feel they should do something else, and it's a real dilemma. Tell him that it isn't that he is inferior. It's just that he's going through a normal stage of life.

GROVE   Yes. Emphasize it as a stage that other people have and get through.

HALEY   Sure. Some men decide to stay with the same old job because it's secure. Others decide to try something different. But everybody has to decide. You force the issue, really. He has to either say, "I'm going to stay the way I am or I'm going to have to change."

GROVE   That makes it so, even if he did stay in the same old job, it wouldn't be him staying there because he's forced to, it would be because he's decided to stay there. It's his decision.

HALEY   That's right, he's asserted himself.

GROVE   He's asserted himself! (*laughs*) That's right. I haven't talked to you about her own family. But I'm less worried about them than I am about her husband.

HALEY   Her father's dead and her mother's alive?

GROVE   Right, and she has a sister. It sounds like my client is the one that everybody calls when they get in trouble. The grandmother sounds like this happy-go-lucky type of woman who has all these boyfriends. She likes to call my client up and tell her, "I've got a boyfriend." The grandmother spends all her money freely, and she won't help her daughter out with the kids. She won't even babysit for her. My client does everything for her mother and her sister, and they don't do anything for her. I wonder if there's something her husband could do to help her with that.

HALEY   He could get the grandmother to babysit more to let them go out. But it would be best if he did something that his wife would find unusual for him to do.

GROVE   If he did something that would be out of character for him, then his wife would be uncertain about him. She might not be so sure that he can't handle her improvement. The hard part is that I have to get *him* to come up with what that might be.

HALEY   I would ask him what her mother thinks of their relationship? Does she think it's a romantic one? I think he'd say, "No, she doesn't think we're very romantic." Then you could suggest that, in front of his mother-in-law, he put his arms around his wife and kiss her. Something that would make the grandmother think they had a romantic relationship. Then he has to think about, "What would she think would be romantic?" He'll begin to think of things that he could do that would be romantic.

GROVE   To think of this man initiating anything is really major.

He seems to be incompetent with the children as a way of trying to keep his wife at home and not working. He just lets them run out of the house and feebly says, "No, don't do that," and they go and do it. She knows he does it on purpose. I talked to her about being sick a week and seeing if he would take charge. I was thinking of her pretending to have the problem.

HALEY Have her stay in bed and let him handle the kids, you mean?

GROVE Yes, but I'm not sure that's the right approach. That's different from trying to get him to initiate something.

HALEY I wonder if you could get him in a mood to prove something to you, something he could do that he would be pleased to tell you about. You're after that kind of a relationship. Like you're coaching him with his wife, only you're coaching him without knowing what to do.

GROVE I coach him from a one-down position where he can come in and either say, "Your idea didn't work, this other thing did," or say, "See, I did this even though you didn't think I could."

HALEY Another way to go is to ask him what he remembers of the last five years that was wonderful that he and his wife did. Then get him started once a month doing it again.

GROVE Help him find something that he's already done, so that it's his idea.

HALEY He must be living a pretty dull life. Working in a job he doesn't like. He probably comes home and watches TV while the kids yell.

Follow-Up

This case had a very successful outcome. After this consultation, I ended up meeting two times alone with the stuck-in-the-mud husband. This man's appearance was so terrible, and his motivation so low, that Haley's suggestion for me to apologize to a man like that was very striking. I did apologize, and it had a powerful effect on my relationship with him. I apologized for helping his wife become so unpredictable. As a way of joining, the two of us had a "male" conversation complaining about how unpredictable women can be. To try to motivate him, I then explained that, now that his wife was improving her life, she would probably expect more from him. I told him that I was worried she might leave him if he could not deliver. We talked about how he has to fight fire with fire, and therefore he could do some unpredictable things himself. He did end up supporting his wife working, although I do not know if this was his unpredictable thing.

I also talked to him about his work dilemma. This man's self-esteem was very low. It was a very helpful idea to frame his lack of motivation to both he and his wife as a difficult midlife crisis, and not as a serious psychopathology. I told him that the positive thing about having a midlife crisis is that, once you make a decision, the crisis will go away. He made a decision to find another job, which he did. This seemed to be the major turning point for this couple.

In addition to the two sessions alone with the husband, I had several more sessions with the couple, focusing on reorganizing their marriage to accommodate the wife's changes. After ending the therapy, I made a follow-up call around three months later and spoke with the wife. She was continuing to work, had lost weight, and felt she was past her depression. Her husband had his new job, with which he seemed pleased. Interestingly, she volunteered to me that she had come off her medicine for her panic attacks. Privately, I took this to mean she and her husband were again having a sexual relationship.

ONE MAN WAS NOT ENOUGH

This is a case in which I consulted behind a one-way mirror as a cotherapist for three live therapy sessions attempting to help a therapist save a case which was not going well. The client was a woman who had chronic depression for many years. The therapist had dedicated himself to helping this client for one year. The client then relapsed and was hospitalized. The therapist took this very hard, feeling he had tried everything he knew to help her. When the client was released from the hospital, she again wanted to see the therapist. At that point the therapist asked me to work with him to try to get a better outcome. Even with my help the case did not turn out well. The conversations with Haley on this case, however, were very valuable and I include them for that reason.

GROVE   The client is a woman in her early forties, married, with one child in middle school and one in high school. The therapist had been seeing this woman for depression and other symptoms, and she relapsed. She made a suicide attempt about two months ago. She overdosed by taking several medications at once and went into the hospital. Now, listen to this, when she was in the hospital, she got nine shock treatments! She was begging them to stop shocking her. They finally did stop, and then said she was uncooperative with the treatment! When she was released from the hospital, her memory loss from the shock treatment was so bad she could not find her way back and forth from her local grocery store!

   The problem is that she's chronically depressed and suicidal. She has other symptoms also. She has eating disorders. She's very very thin and she thinks she's overweight. It's a constant struggle to get her to stay at a weight that's reasonable. On top of all of that, this lady has been in therapy forever. This wasn't her first hospitalization. Before she saw this therapist she was in a famous inpatient setting for a long period of time. Before that, she was with some other doctor for a year. Being a patient is a lifestyle for her.

   Since she returned home from the hospital the therapist has seen her four times alone, with the goal of getting her back on her feet and eliminating her suicidal ideation. We've asked her to bring her husband and she refuses. We made an agreement for the therapist to see her four times alone and if she did not improve we would insist on her husband coming to sessions.

Right now we're concentrating on getting her back on her feet. She doesn't do anything. She doesn't work. She just sits at home all day thinking about suicide.

HALEY   What's your hypothesis about why she's behaving this way?

GROVE   I think it has to do with her marriage. Her husband is a salesman on commission and he doesn't make enough money. I've never met him, but he sounds like a wayward soul to me. He sounds like this real polite man who will come in and be all agreeable and everything but he's a lost soul. The therapist doesn't agree with that, but every time he describes the man, he sounds like that to me.

HALEY   Has the therapist met him?

GROVE   Yes. Before the client was hospitalized, the therapist had her parents in and he's had the husband in. During the course of the year the therapist has seen all these different family members.

I think the problem is the marriage because, when she was in the hospital, the hospital staff had her saying that she would leave her husband.

HALEY   They encouraged her to say that?

GROVE   While she was in the hospital getting shock treatment, the staff encouraged her to separate from her husband. Make sense out of that. In that kind of situation, this lady is supposed to make a decision like that. That just sounded too suspicious to me. She relapses, goes into the hospital, and then we're talking about her separating from her husband. Then when she got out she was struggling with what to do and she decided to stay in the marriage. But she presents it as a death sentence, "Oh, I'll just stay."

I think the problem is the marriage, and I think if she gets better the husband is going to have a problem. That's what I'm worried about. But she is so protective of this man that she won't let him come to therapy. The therapist wants to help the client uncover the root cause of her problem. He tries to ask her questions like: "Would your husband get upset if you did this or did that?" She's so protective of him, she always says, "No, it's all my problem, it's not his, it's all me." So my hypothesis is that it's the marriage. But we've had this agreement with her to see her alone for four times and we've been giving her directives intended to motivate her and get her back on her feet.

If we help her to the point where she goes back to work, I think we're going to have problems. She relapsed right after she began a good job. I think this lady wants a lifestyle where she can stay home and take care of the kids. But her husband does not have a job that can support that. It's a struggle between him and the wife.

HALEY You present this like you have a problem with the colleague you're working with.

GROVE One problem is that he took her relapse pretty hard.

HALEY I think it might help to say to your therapist that, as people with serious symptoms improve, they often have one relapse. At least I've been finding that, particularly with the very crazy clients. We sometimes get one hospitalization before they're out of it. I think it's a mistake to take that as, "Well, my God, now we start over. . . . We did it wrong." Sometimes a relapse seems to be part of the process toward improving.

GROVE This is a difficult lady to work with. She's been in therapy for years and she wants to have insight. She's interested in the "cause" of her problem, even though that's the style of therapy she's been getting for years and it hasn't worked.

HALEY Does her husband have a girlfriend?

GROVE I don't know. I don't think so, but that's a good question. Why? Because she has a therapist, is that what you're thinking?

HALEY Because the therapist is on her side and you have to have symmetry. The husband might be joined with the kids. He must have somebody. You see a lot of cases of salesmen who aren't good salesmen and aren't making a living. Some of them hide out. They spend their afternoon in bars, instead of selling. He may be that kind of a man. If they have a pattern where she's overresponsible and he's irresponsible, then they have a problem.

GROVE We asked her what she would be doing if she didn't have her symptoms. She described a lifestyle of volunteering at the school with the kids and doing her hobbies at home. When she relapsed she wanted out of her job. She hated that job.

HALEY Did you find out why she did not want to go to work that last day?

GROVE No. She'd been complaining about her work for a period of time and trying to get the therapist to write her a letter saying that she shouldn't work because of psychological problems. He wouldn't do it. Then she relapsed.

HALEY It sounds like, if she works and does well, her husband doesn't do anything.

GROVE Yes, that's what I'm worried about. But what do you do with that? Get her back on her feet and see what happens?

HALEY You can put him in charge of her improving. I wouldn't let her block the husband's coming in. That's letting her decide how the therapy is to be done.

GROVE Right, that's what's happening. She is just adamant about keeping him out of therapy. I was thinking that we could go with seeing her alone if she keeps improving, and if she doesn't get better we can then be more insistent about her husband's attendance.

HALEY It sounds like she doesn't think your therapist can handle her husband. Any woman who's adamant about her husband not coming in, who is protective of him anyhow, is protective of her husband in relation to the therapy. She's concerned that the therapist is going to probe and upset him, something like that.

GROVE But they've had sessions before.

HALEY   They got along OK?

GROVE   As far as I know they did. The husband complained they
don't have enough sex and the therapist sided with him on
that.
      So you'd put him in charge of helping her to improve. Well,
I think that's the obvious thing to do. My idea with the suicidal
thoughts was to have the husband sit with her every day and
have her tell him all the suicidal thoughts she had that day.

HALEY   I'd make it broader than that. I would tell the husband,
"She's just recovering from the attempted suicide and being in
the hospital. She needs help getting on her feet." Then I would
have *him* describe how she would be if everything was going
well.

GROVE   *He* should describe that? *His* description is going to be
different than *hers*. He's going to way, "She should be working."
She doesn't want that.

HALEY   He'll say she should be working, and taking care of the
house, and cleaning the house, and providing more sex.

GROVE   (*laughs*). Right. Well, if he says, "She should be working,"
should we say, "But she doesn't want to work. What if that's
not in HER plan for recovery?"

HALEY   I wouldn't deal with that.

GROVE   Why?

HALEY   Because you're going by *his* judgment of what she needs.

GROVE   You would trust his judgment over hers?

HALEY   I would want him to say, "She should be working," and
her to say, "I shouldn't be working." Then it's between them.
You shouldn't get in there and say, "She won't work."

GROVE   Right.

HALEY   She has to refuse to work.

GROVE   Which she won't say out loud because she's one of these
typical psychosomatic clients who just lets her symptoms do
her talking. She won't say out loud, "I don't want to work."

HALEY Well, if she says she's going to work, she should work.

GROVE I like this. Tell me if you think this fits in. We've been talking to her about her need to express herself with her mouth instead of with her body.

HALEY Sure.

GROVE She needs to start saying the things that she wants and doesn't want. She agrees that she should do that and I think we should tell the husband that. One of her problems is that she doesn't say what she really wants.

HALEY I would do it a little differently. I would say that some women can be planning to do something and then not do it because they have a headache. Those women have to have a real headache. Other women can say they have a headache and not have to have a real headache. Your client needs help saying that she's unwell. When she's feeling OK she still might want to get out of things. Her problem is she's so honest that she has to actually feel a pain to get out of something. If you put it to the couple like that, you introduce an uncertainty. When she says to him she can't do something, he won't know whether she really has a problem or not.

GROVE Say that again, because that's tricky. Let me see if I can say it. She needs help. Some women actually need a headache to get out of something. Other women can say they have one and not really have one.

HALEY Some women actually have to have it, yes.

GROVE Some women have to have it so that they're being honest.

HALEY Right, and some can just say, "I have a headache," and get out of something.

GROVE She's the honest kind. She needs help.

HALEY She's a psychosomatic person. She has to actually feel it.

GROVE She has to feel it. You're accepting her whole need to have a symptom.

HALEY Sure. But she shouldn't have to suffer while she's doing it.

GROVE This is where it gets tricky. When you say she shouldn't
have to suffer, you're saying she shouldn't actually have to have
a headache. Is that what you're saying?

HALEY Sure. Or since she also has a problem with weight, she
could gain some weight and keep it secret, and still say she was
underweight, and so on.

GROVE (*laughs*) That's great!

HALEY She doesn't have to be honest about herself.

GROVE Let me make sure I understand this. What you're going
after is the honesty of it.

HALEY You're after uncertainty.

GROVE You're trying to create an uncertainty where he's not sure
whether she actually has a headache or not, or whether this is
just a game. So you're changing that aspect of it. Well, I'm just
trying to figure out how you get that across in a way that
makes sense.

HALEY The husband of a psychosomatic person is always uncertain. Is there really something wrong with her, or isn't there?
Because psychosomatic means there's nothing wrong, but
there is.

GROVE Right! But you just increase that uncertainty?

HALEY That's right.

GROVE Why would you increase that?

HALEY Because then it undermines her ability to use that.

GROVE Oh, I see.

HALEY So he will say, "For God's sakes, you should go to work
whether you feel bad or not! I have to go to work whether I
feel bad or not."

GROVE Oh! I understand. If she wakes up one day and says, "I'm
depressed and I don't want to go to work," their normal argument is whether she's actually depressed or not.

HALEY That's right.

GROVE You're changing that into the argument that it doesn't matter if you're depressed. You're getting him to accept her statement, but she has to live life anyway. That's what you're changing.

HALEY Well, you're also introducing an uncertainty. If in his presence, you say to her, "You don't have to feel depressed in order to be able to get out of things because you're depressed. If you learn how to be untruthful, you can say you're depressed and then not have to do whatever's required of you."

GROVE What if he says, "Why would she want to be untruthful? Why should she learn how to be untruthful, why is that important?"

HALEY Then you need to say, "Well, your wife shouldn't have to suffer."

GROVE (laughs)

HALEY Right?

GROVE You don't want her to suffer just because she needs a little excuse to get out of doing something. I see! That's great.

HALEY I would think of it in the same way as an agoraphobic wife, with the husband jealous if the wife improves and goes out somewhere.

GROVE Right, I understand that one.

HALEY You do the same thing, only around this woman's depression. What can he do to help her not get depressed? For example, you tell them, as a couple, that people get over depression when they have to take action or when they get angry. You can't be angry and depressed at the same time. If he would make her do things so that she would begin to get angry, then she would feel better.

GROVE Tell me what that's going to produce.

HALEY He either will collapse or assert himself more, so that she can be better.

GROVE Take me through this. I think that if she goes back to work again, that's when he'll really get to be a wayward soul. We need to be prepared for that possibility.

HALEY   You can work with them together on that. You can say couples have rules. In their case they seem to have the rule that she's supposed to be responsible at certain times, and he's supposed to be irresponsible at certain times. Once she starts going to work and becomes more responsible, he will have to balance that. So, could they plan in advance that he's going to be irresponsible the day she goes to work?

GROVE   Make a paradox. The thing is, it's not out in the open that he's doing that.

HALEY   Well, first you get the income he's providing.

GROVE   They have serious money problems.

HALEY   So, then he has to be more responsible than she. If they have serious money problems, then he should have two jobs.

GROVE   Yes.

HALEY   She'd rather he had two jobs than she have one job.

GROVE   That's exactly right. But she won't say that. She won't say, "Why aren't you earning more? Why can't you get yourself together?" She won't say that in a million years. Instead she says, "It's all my problem, my depression and all this hardship I'm causing."

HALEY   Sure. Well, then I would say he has to help her. She doesn't want the problem to be the marriage. She doesn't want it said that the husband is the problem. There's where you have to work within the framework of her having the problem.

GROVE   Right, and that's why she doesn't want her husband to come in. That's the mistake the therapist made before. I think you're right, she's protecting him from the therapist. The therapist tried to make it explicit that they had marital problems. I'm sure that upset this couple.

HALEY   Because that means he's going to make interpretations to them.

GROVE Right. I think you're telling me what I already know. Get the husband in, put him in charge, and see what happens.

HALEY You know, working with psychotic wives who are absolutely out of their minds, the solution is to work with the husband and get him to not put up with the wife's crazy behavior. The moment he doesn't put up with it, the wife becomes more normal.

GROVE All right, that's great. That's exactly what I needed. The guideline is getting him to say he doesn't want to put up with her depression anymore.

HALEY When you put him charge of doing something about it, and then she doesn't collaborate, he gets angry and says, "I won't put up with this."

GROVE So you try to get her to provoke him to say, "I won't put up with it."

HALEY Sure. You get these passive guys, and they have a crazy wife. Working with the wife alone won't help, and working with the couple focusing on their marriage won't help. Having the husband do something about his wife, especially in relation to his rights, is what helps.

GROVE Right. I understand. This thing about getting him to put his foot down puts it all in perspective.

HALEY If you frame it as a marital problem, you're saying it's the husband's fault.

GROVE Right. The wife won't go along with that.

Six Weeks Later

GROVE This is a follow-up to the case of the chronically depressed wife. There are a lot of new developments. I didn't know this the last time we talked, but after she got out of the hospital she got herself involved with a minister, enlisting him to help her with her problems. She drove out of state to see him. She struck up a personal relationship with this man. Now, one of our problems is that she's constantly calling him and he is advising her on the phone. This minister called us and said, "I don't want her calling me. You guys take her!" But he won't tell her, "Stop calling me." He's worried she'll get depressed and kill herself if he does that. It's one of our very serious problems right now because she thinks that we're trying to take the minister away from her. She's mad at the therapist for that. The minister won't take himself out of the picture. He's too nice.

HALEY   Did she see him, or just talk to him?

GROVE   She's seen him, and now she calls him up all the time.

HALEY   But she isn't visiting him.

GROVE   No. He lives in another area. But she calls him.

Another major development is that we finally got the husband to come in with her and it was an extraordinary session. For the first 15 minutes, he yelled at the therapist for all the bad things the therapist has done to his wife. The husband's mad because we're making her do therapy in front of a one way mirror. He's also mad that when she was in the hospital she desperately wanted the therapist to go visit her and he wouldn't do it. She and her husband thought that was the cruelest thing anybody could ever do, not visit her in the hospital. Now on top of all of that, the therapist is trying to take this minister away.

HALEY   I think they are right. The therapist should have visited her in the hospital. I think the therapist should always visit when a client is in the hospital. Not to do therapy necessarily, but to just pay a social visit.

GROVE   I agree completely. I took that position with the therapist and suggested he should apologize to them for not visiting. He had a different position on that issue and he would not apologize. He was concerned that the woman was too dependent on him and visiting her in the hospital would only magnify that dependence.

My plan for the session was for the husband to come in and for us to organize him around helping her. What happened instead was that he came in and it looked like these two men, the husband and the therapist, were arguing over this woman. It gave me the impression that for the last year she has been seeing this therapist alone, and then when she would go home her husband would ask, "How did your therapy go?" She would say, "He did this and he did that." That would then organize the husband to be on her side and pay attention to her. If you didn't know who anybody was, if you were to just look at these three people talking, it would look like two men arguing over a woman, and her sitting there loving it!

We set up several things in this session. I wanted to set up something where the husband could help the wife. For example, in the evening, when he comes home we asked them to sit down together, and she's to tell him all of her suicidal thoughts. He's to listen to her compassionately. They're also to keep a chart together so that when they come in we can know whether she's improving or not. I gave them these ridiculous directives, hoping that they would do something else. I wanted to hear what you thought about how I set this up, in terms of the directives we gave in this session.

HALEY In what you're having them do, what will cheer the woman or the husband up?

GROVE Well, I think she wants more from him. But I'm not sure. It's either that, or he's putting up with this because she threatens to leave him, and he's afraid if he takes a stand he might lose her.

HALEY When wives get depressed, often it means that they want to leave, but they can't.

GROVE I'm not sure if he's putting up with this and she would improve if only he would just say, "Look, you have to straighten up."

HALEY You know, there are two things about him. I think if you have the hypothesis that she's holding him up in some way by her depression then you put him in charge of helping her and she'll cooperate with that.

GROVE Right.

HALEY But to help her, he has to help her do something that's more interesting than sitting around being depressed. Just talking about the depression will only make her more depressed.

GROVE OK.

HALEY To both of them together I would say that because she is into a depressing routine, the two of them should do something this weekend they've never done before. Or that they don't think they'll like.

GROVE Why that they don't think they'll like?

HALEY Because then they might do it. (*laughs*) They may not do it if you asked them to do something they would like.

GROVE How would you tell them?

HALEY Well, you say to them, "I'd like you to pick something that you really don't think would interest you, and yet it might, but you don't think it would. Like going out on the river in a rowboat. You probably don't think that would be nice for you. But, think it over, and decide on something that you think probably you wouldn't like."

GROVE What if they say, "How come you want us to do something that we think we wouldn't like to do?"

HALEY "Because you want to expand your wife's horizons. When she does only what she likes it's depressing because she's in that frame of mind. She has to get out of that frame of mind."

GROVE You would say, "Because the depression makes her confused"?

HALEY Whatever she can think of now that seems reasonable to her is within the framework of her being depressed.

GROVE It sounds like you're getting them together as a couple with that. You're assuming that's what she wants.

HALEY Sure. Or that it's cheering her up by doing something besides sitting around being depressed.

GROVE When would you assume that it's like these other couples where the husband is putting up with wife's symptoms and she improves if the husband finally says, "By God! I'm not going to put up with this anymore."

HALEY Well, that's when the wife is psychotic more than depressed. When she's behaving randomly, really.

GROVE When she's behaving randomly, you assume that the husband needs to take a stand.

HALEY Yes.

GROVE If it's depression, you assume what?

HALEY Well, I assume he has to pull himself together to help her, and guide her, and get exasperated with her, and so on. But he doesn't have to fight for his life, like if she were crazy. With a depressed wife, I would assume the husband has some depressive problems, or she wouldn't be doing this. With depression you have to get some life in the marriage. There's another thing that's obvious. You may not be thinking it because it's so obvious. She could be trying to get away from him.

GROVE I know! I can't tell if she wants to be closer to him or away from him. I'm confused about what she wants.

HALEY She's not only trying to get her husband better, but she's struggling with the therapist like she has to have a boyfriend. Not an affair, necessarily, but a male friend.

GROVE I think the therapist has been the third person, stabilizing the marriage. She has resisted so strongly having the husband come to therapy. I thought it was because maybe when the therapist had him in before, he upset him. Now, after seeing this session, I think it's that she's had this game where she has this other man on the side. Bringing them together takes that away from her.

HALEY I would assume her husband neglects her. When she gets involved in something, or mentions the therapist, the husband comes out and competes, treating her better.

GROVE   Right. That's what I saw behind the mirror. The two men fighting over her. That's exactly what I saw behind the mirror.

HALEY   She would only do that if her husband were neglecting her.

GROVE   That's what I came away with from that session, but I didn't think of the obvious thing, to arrange for him to pay more attention to her.

HALEY   By doing something that may not interest them.

GROVE   Why are you proposing that?

HALEY   They're in an unhappy framework at the moment. They should get out of that and into a new framework. To do that, they'd have to think about doing something that they probably wouldn't ordinarily think of and perhaps not even like. Like, they could take a boating trip.

GROVE   You think that if I ask them to do something they won't like, they will spontaneously come up with something else which they ordinarily wouldn't think of.

HALEY   They will refuse, but they'll go into a different category of some kind of entertainment. They'll stay in the same class. That's an Erickson theory.

GROVE   Explain that.

HALEY   The classic Erickson case is a woman who couldn't even read a book because her 50-year-old son would bother her constantly.[2]

GROVE   (laughs) A 50-year-old son! She already has a pretty serious problem.

HALEY   (laughs) Well, he described it like a 50-year-old son bothering his mother. The son was psychotic. Erickson told her to drive her son out in the desert and push him out of the car. She was stronger than he was. She was to push him out into that hot sun. Then she should drive a mile, and she should park the car and sit and read a book. He would yell and scream and stamp his feet, but it's hot out there. The only place he can go is to her. He would have to walk that mile, and she would get half an hour or an hour reading the book comfortably in the car.

GROVE Right. With him out following her. (*laughter*) That's great! He sold her on it because she could get a half hour of reading in peace.

HALEY That's right. Afterwards, the son began to walk faster, to get out of that hot sun.

GROVE But, what do you mean by a different class?

HALEY This is what I'm getting to. After a few days of doing this, the son didn't like it at all. The son came to Erickson with his mother and said, "Couldn't I choose a different exercise? I've been·walking out in this hot sun. What about bowling? I could practice bowling while my mother sits and reads a book." Erickson said, "OK."

GROVE I see. So, you give them an absurd thing, and then they shift. They keep some aspect of what you give, but shift to a more normal thing on their own.

HALEY Erickson said, if you pick an item in a class and they don't want to do that item, they'll do another, but they'll stay within the class.

GROVE They'll stay within the class, but they'll pick their own item.

HALEY The son didn't want to walk in the desert to exercise, but he didn't rebel into non-exercise. He rebelled into a different exercise.

GROVE So, with this couple we have to give them something that they won't like, so they'll pick something that they do like.

HALEY That's right.

GROVE The one I'm stuck on is the rationale for asking them to do something they aren't going to like.

HALEY I think you can say to the husband that if he picks something he thought his wife didn't like, he'd be surprised. I think he's competing with your therapist, so he'll say, "I won't be surprised." He'll want to prove the therapist wrong.

GROVE He'll do it and then they'll say, "We don't like your idea. We should do this other thing."

HALEY Or, they'll come in and say, "We did your lousy thing, and it didn't help a bit. But the next time we'll do something of our own choice."

GROVE Right.

HALEY You have to get something going between them besides depression. Whatever they're doing now depresses them. Just having him help her experience the depression isn't sufficient.

GROVE Right.

HALEY Does the minister call the therapist?

GROVE Yes. The minister calls the therapist and says, "She's calling me again! What do I do?" The therapist said, "Look, you have to tell her not to call you." The minister said, "But if I do, she'll commit suicide or get depressed." This is a man who was depressed himself at one time.

HALEY The minister?

GROVE Yes. He's thinking, "She must be as bad as I was, and if someone who was helping me would have rejected me back then, I would have killed myself." So he can't tell her, "Don't call me." But she calls him five times a day and says things like, "I drove my car, and I almost drove into a telephone pole, what do I do?" He says, "My God! I don't want this woman telling me all this." But then he doesn't say, "Don't call me, call your therapist."

HALEY I would ask him to misunderstand her.

GROVE To what?

HALEY To misunderstand her. He could tell her something that isn't appropriate, or that won't help her. That is, if she says, "I've been thinking about killing myself," he should ask her to say a prayer about how important parents are, or something like that.

GROVE   So that he doesn't have to feel like he's rejecting her. She'll reject him, instead of him rejecting her.

HALEY   Right. Tell him it's important that she disengage from him, rather than having him disengage from her.

GROVE   That's a very good way.

HALEY   He'll succeed if he benevolently misunderstands her in some way. It might be hard for him to do that, but if you get him interested he might do it.

GROVE   I like that a lot. I didn't think of that. I hope we haven't lost this case already. I like the different class idea. That's a hard concept to grasp.

HALEY   That took some effort for me to understand, too. I'm writing a paper on Erickson, and I use that example. Obviously, he had put some thought into the problem of therapy being changing people's classification systems and that the way you change it is not by going against it. You go with one part of it, and then they spontaneously make a new choice of their own.

GROVE   You go with part of their classification system, then they pick something else, that is still a part of the class you gave them. You accept their framework while at the same time expanding their horizons.

HALEY   Surely. You know, you can test it. I bet if you told that couple to go to a bad little theater group and see a play this coming Friday just so they'd have the experience of criticizing, I think they'd go to a good play. Or a good movie.

GROVE   Something that will upset her. Here's a way—a depressing play, that will help her understand her depression! Because she wants insight. I say, "This will help you understand. You'll get some ideas about your depression if you go to some depressing plays. Because you'll be able to relate to some of the characters, and you'll see things in the characters."

HALEY   That sounds too rational. You just tell them to go to a bad play.

GROVE   You keep telling me I'm too rational, but I struggle with giving an absurd directive without some rational reason for giving it. You're saying I don't need a rational reason. Just give it.

HALEY   With some people you don't. With others, you have to explain, and be rational, and all that. But, in an antagonistic situation, like your therapist is in with this man, anything that he suggests, the man has to do something else.

GROVE   Yes.

HALEY   So it's a matter of what to choose to ask him to do that will cause him to stay within that class and do something else. If you want him to take his wife out for a pleasant evening at a play, you ask him to take her out to a bad play.

GROVE   Right.

HALEY   But you might not do that with another person.

Follow-Up

After the last session with the wife and her husband together, the woman decided she wanted to seek advice from the minister exclusively. She dropped out of therapy. The therapist and the minister then kept in touch periodically over the next few months, as several dramatic events unfolded. A few months after the woman stopped seeing the therapist she called him up in great distress. She had separated from her husband and he had become very depressed. As she spoke to the therapist by phone, her husband was standing next to her. She said he was not eating, or sleeping, and was very despondent. It seemed that the couple had switched with each other on who was having the symptoms. The wife wanted help from the therapist in getting her husband hospitalized.

The therapist asked to speak to the husband. The husband told him that he was not depressed; in fact he was fine. The therapist checked with the couple's insurance company and found that for the man to be hospitalized a face-to-face assessment would have to first be conducted. The husband was scheduled to be seen two days later. Before he could be assessed, he made a suicide attempt. Later, the minister talked by phone to the husband, and the husband dismissed his suicide attempt as not very serious. The couple never did return to therapy.

A few weeks later the therapist learned that the wife was indeed separated from the husband and that she had a boyfriend with whom she was very involved. She continued to have two men, only now it was a boyfriend and her husband, instead of a therapist and her husband. This is the last the therapist heard about this couple. It is not known if they got back together or if they divorced.

Discussion

GROVE   A common presenting problem is a couple where one of the spouses has a symptom. I was trying to think if anyone has ever tried to classify marital contracts according to the symptoms that one of the spouses might have. In other words, if a wife is depressed, what are the interpersonal characteristics of that marriage? If a wife has psychosomatic symptoms, or if a husband is irresponsible, what are the interpersonal characteristics of that marriage? You see what I mean?

HALEY   Yes.

GROVE   As we've had these consultations, it has become clear to me that you have a set of premises that goes along with each of those types of marriages. If you have an agoraphobic wife, you already have an idea about what you expect could be going on there.

HALEY   Sure.

GROVE   You already have ideas about what characteristics go along with each type of marriage. I thought we might go through a few examples.

HALEY   It would be better if you said a wife with geographical limitations, or a suicidal wife. I prefer not to use the technical terminology, but to use what they do — or threaten to do — instead.

GROVE   OK. I was thinking, for example, about a "geographically limited" wife who cannot leave her house. You start by assuming that she's stuck at home, but she's fantasizing about leaving the marriage. She worries that if she goes out of the house, her husband is going to be insecure about that, and the couple will become unstable.

HALEY   Right. When I was in practice, I had a sample once of five agoraphobic wives. One of the things that was common was that, besides having anxiety when she would leave the house, the wife was also anxious even when she was at home. The husband had to be available to her at all time, even while he was at work. He had to be right by a phone all day long. He couldn't go out to lunch. He had to sit at his desk in case she got anxious and had to call him.

GROVE   What do you think was the basis for that?

HALEY   I think she was restricting him by having her anxiety. Just as he was restricting her by reacting if she went outside the house alone.

GROVE   Jealousy is a major theme when agoraphobia is a problem. I didn't realize that it went both ways. I already knew that the husband of an agoraphobic woman typically becomes jealous if his wife goes out, but I didn't realize the jealousy went both ways. I see a woman who has serious anxiety when she leaves the house. With that couple you're absolutely right; she's madly jealous about her husband, too. She got furious with him because he told her about a woman at work and she thought he knew too many details about this woman. It's a woman with whom her husband has worked for 15 years. She was upset that he could possibly know what he knows about this woman.

HALEY She's jealous that he knows those intimate things.

GROVE She thinks he shouldn't know them, right? The intimate details that he shouldn't know are things like how many kids the woman has, whether her family went on a summer vacation or not. That's too intimate! It's true; with that couple jealousy is a major aspect, both ways.

HALEY It's a contract.

GROVE What is the contract?

HALEY Well, she agrees to stay home if he keeps her aware of where he is at all times. He can only come straight home from work because she might get anxious. He can't dillydally. He can't go out in the evening because she'd get anxious. What impressed me with these couples was that often, the husband couldn't even go out to lunch. He had to have a bag lunch at his desk by the phone, in case she got anxious at home alone.

GROVE You and I have talked about a procedure where the husband is put in charge of helping the wife over her anxiety. The wife makes a list of all of the places she can't go without having anxiety and then the husband is directed to take her to those places to desensitize her. How does that procedure resolve that jealousy contract?

HALEY Well, you do other things besides have him take her places. You also talk to them about their marriage and various things while he's doing this. You talk about marital issues as an aside topic. Usually, if you put the husband in charge of expanding her range geographically, he then lets her go as far as *he* can tolerate her going. He'll change while the therapist is helping the wife expand her range geographically.

GROVE Without the husband going out with her?

HALEY Right.

GROVE In other words, she drops her jealousy if he drops his jealousy.

HALEY It seems to happen that way.

GROVE Oh! I see! It's a contract that, "By God! If you're going to make me stay home, I'm going to keep an eye on you every second of the day."

HALEY "You're not going to be out enjoying yourself while I'm home."

GROVE If he then lets her out enjoying herself, she will reciprocate.

HALEY Right. What I arranged was that the husband not have lunch at the desk one day, to make sure his wife could tolerate an hour of anxiety without being able to contact him if she were upset. Then you begin to get a little separation. He gets some time where she doesn't know where he is and she gets some time out of the house when he doesn't know where she is.

GROVE You have to work on both sides of the jealousy at once, basically.

HALEY But you stay within the framework of the wife being anxious. The wife does not want it said that her husband is jealous, or insecure, so out of respect for her you stay within the framework that she is presenting to you. She has this anxiety.

GROVE I didn't recognize the importance of jealousy as a general theme.

HALEY Right. It helps to realize that usually the jealousy can work both ways.

3 | VIOLENCE

GROVE This is a case of a man who has been violent towards his wife for most of their 16-year-marriage. The husband is 38 years old. The wife is 39. They have three kids, a six-year-old boy, a 12-year-old girl and a 15-year-old girl. It's the only marriage for each.

It's a classic batterer situation. She can't tell him anything that might upset him. He's very jealous and possessive. If she leaves the house it has to be in secret. One day recently she snuck off to buy something for one of her daughters while her husband was at work. When the husband came home from work the son told the father that his mom had gone out. The husband proceeded to punch her in the face and beat her up pretty badly.

The next day, after the husband went to work, she took all the children and went to the shelter. That was the first time she'd ever tried to leave him by going to a shelter. He'd been beating her the whole marriage but after this time she couldn't take it anymore. He came home for lunch and found that no one was home. They don't have a phone, so he went back to work and called around to relatives. When he realized she had left him, he got a gun from his car and locked himself in an office at his workplace, threatening to shoot himself. The police were called and came to try to calm him down. He then got into a six-hour struggle with the police, with him barricaded inside this office holding a gun to his head, making very serious threats, and the police outside trying to coax him out. When he finally came out he was arrested for domestic violence and public disorderly conduct and put in jail. The court took the children from the mother and put them in foster care, arguing that she couldn't protect them from him. I got this case with the kids in foster care, the man in jail and unemployed, the wife living alone in their home, and the community scared to death of this man.

First let me tell you what I've done so far. I've had several sessions with the mother alone. I've also had one session involving her mother and three sisters to set up a plan for her family to protect her from violence. He's been out of jail now for about one month. I have kept the couple separated. I have her connected with her family and him living with his parents. He still has to go back to court to face these charges, so right now we're in an in-between time waiting for his guilt or innocence to be decided by the court.

HALEY   Has he ever harmed the children?

GROVE   He hasn't ever harmed the children. The wife said that, he said that, and the kids said that.

HALEY   But they've been taken away from their mother because he might do something to them?

GROVE   The argument is he might hurt her and they might get caught in the cross fire. The worst thing that I know of that he's done was to point a loaded gun at her during an argument and threaten to shoot her. Over the course of their marriage he has apparently done that several times. The children told me about that. My biggest fear is that she'll go back to him and he'll harm her. Or she'll leave him for good and he'll blow his brains out. It's very serious.

HALEY Right now they haven't decided if they will get back together or not?

GROVE No.

HALEY You've seen him alone and her alone?

GROVE Yes. Originally she decided to leave him, but then she
wavered and now she isn't sure what to do. She loves him and
wants the marriage to work out, but she's terrified of him. For
a while there he was pressuring her to lie when they go to
court and say that he didn't hit her. I told her that's a sign that
she can't trust him. For her to trust him, one thing he has to
do is take responsibility for what he's done. I told him alone,
"You have to be honest in court. She doesn't trust you right
now and if you want her to trust you, you have to be honest
about what you did."

She says she's watching him and if he straightens up she'll
take him back. She wants to stay with him, but she doesn't
want the violence. She says if he ever hits her again she's leaving
him for good. Since he's been out of jail he's been treating her
all right. She's not sure, though, if that's just because he has to
go in front of a judge. But she wants to work it out. That is
what she says alone. My position with her is, "Look, I'm not
trying to tell you one way or the other what to do. But you
know him. You're the one who's at risk."

He says he wants her back and can barely stand it that
they're separated. I told him, "You've lost her. If you want to
get her back you have to win her trust back because she's afraid
of you. If you want her back then you have to treat her in a
way that she won't be afraid of you."

HALEY How many times have you seen each of them?

GROVE I've seen him three times. Once with his mother, once by
himself, and once with his wife.

HALEY Were they seeing each other on their own anyway?

GROVE Yes. She goes over and sees him at his mother's house.

HALEY   That's important.

GROVE   At one point I had a session with the wife and her mother
and three sisters. I told them, "I would not advise that she see
him, but if she wants to she should not see him by herself.
One or more of you have to go with her." I tried to set it up
for her family to protect her.

The session with the couple together scared me. He was
pressuring me to have a joint meeting with him and his wife. I
asked her if she wanted to meet with him and she said she did.
I asked her to think about what conditions she wanted him to
meet for her to take him back. His idea was: "She's seeing
me so she must not be afraid of me anymore." Really what's
happening is she's just not telling him what's on her mind
because she's very afraid of him.

HALEY   Is she afraid that if she tries to leave him he'll get her?

GROVE   She's afraid of what his reaction would be if she did have
to leave him. The shelter was advising her to relocate secretly
in some other town if she did have to leave him for good. I'm
very worried that plan would not work out in the long run.
This little boy loves his dad and is going crazy in foster care
because he is not able to see his dad. If she's somewhere in
another town with this six-year-old boy never seeing his dad,
that's going to be very hard. If they do separate I wish it could
be from a mutual agreement. His parents could take him in if
he and his wife separate. That's what I'm hoping for, but the
wife's wishy-washy.

Before I brought the two of them together, I told her alone,
"You have to tell him what your true conditions are for you
to take him back. He has to know what the truth is." Then I
brought them together and I took all of the precautions. I had
them talk one at a time and look only at me. I was very
cautious. But that interview was very difficult to control because this man is so damn extreme. She would say, "I need
some time right now. I'm not ready to just get back with you.
I'd like to just see you once in a while, but not live together

for right now." His response was, "Well, I might as well just give up on everything then. Everything's lost. It's useless." He implied he would kill himself. He goes to that extreme.

HALEY   He assumes a partial separation will finish it.

GROVE   Right. Then he doesn't have anything. He might as well end everything. To protect his wife, I had her leave the session early, with him staying with me for a while. Then he played these mind games with me. He had learned that if he says he's suicidal, or if he says he's going to hurt somebody, then I have the authority to put him in the hospital. So he was saying things to me like, "I know what I can and can't say. You can't put me anywhere because I'm not going to hurt anybody." But then he'd say, "But I just don't know what I might do." He said things like that. I ended the session by saying, "Look, I'm very concerned about you and I'm not letting you out of here without at least calling your mother and telling her that you're upset and that she has to watch you." He said, "You don't have a right to do that." I said, "I don't care, I'm doing it anyway." That's what I did and he left mad.

HALEY   His mother came over?

GROVE   No, he stormed out. In hindsight, I should have called her and had her come over. Instead, I called her after he left and said, "He's very upset. I think you should keep an eye on him today." She said, "He's not upset at all. He's sitting in the backyard talking with my husband." That made me think he was just trying to upset me by implying he might harm himself.

This is also important. After I sent the wife out I stayed with him for 45 minutes before I let him go. But, the wife left and came back! When he left, she was in the waiting room waiting for him! When she saw him leaving all mad, her immediate response was to get up and follow him! I had to step in there and block her or she would have gone with him.

After all of this, I decided that if I'm going to work with this man I want some conditions. He's going to have to agree to the conditions or I don't think I can help him. I thought of

four conditions I wanted from him. I told him that I would
help him try to fix his marriage if he wants help doing that. I
said, "If you want to try to fix this your way, you go right
ahead. But I think your way is terrifying your wife. You're not
going to get her back that way. If you want me to help you
with your marriage I'll try to help you, but I have four conditions that you have to agree to. The conditions are:

"1. If I ask you to bring other family members in, for example,
    your parents, you will bring them.
"2. If you say anything to me during the course of a session that
    makes me even suspect that you're thinking about hurting
    yourself or someone else—even if you don't go so far as to
    say that you're going to hurt anyone—I have the right to call
    other family members.
"3. You must conduct yourself in a reasonable manner with your
    children."

   The children are all worried about their parents. The last
impression they all have of him is from the day he had the gun
to his head. They aren't allowed to see him right now, so they
are all in foster care terrified about what condition he's in
psychologically. I'm trying to organize a therapy session with
the children and their father so he can reassure them. Originally
he agreed with me that he would do that. Then, the day he
was upset with me, he said, "I don't think I will see the children,
I don't know what I might say."

"4. You have to turn in all of your guns to the police."

   He has several guns at his house and his wife and kids are
all nervous about his having them after all that has happened.
   I presented him with these conditions and he agreed to meet
them all. My biggest fear is that he is just playing along with
all of this and if his wife goes back to him she'll be in serious
danger. I don't know how to size that up.

HALEY You described an incident that I bet is a metaphor for the history of their marriage. She leaves; 45 minutes later he leaves and she's waiting in the waiting room for him. I bet they have a pattern where she leaves and then comes back. She leaves and yet tempts him. That is part of the violence.

GROVE I asked them what they usually fight about, and they said a lot of it's over money. She gets the bills and she keeps them a secret from him. She's afraid to show him the electric bill because he'll get violent.

HALEY What does he do for a living?

GROVE He had a good job but they let him go because he was threatening people. He lost that job about a year and a half ago and got his most recent job, which he does not like. She says when he lost the job he liked, he got a lot worse. He's been hitting her for 15 years, but he went downhill after he lost that job. There was more tension around the house and he was harder to deal with. His explanation for all of his behavior is that he was a drug addict.

HALEY On what?

GROVE He said he smoked crack cocaine, he smoked marijuana, he drank, and he took various pills. She says she knows he drank, but she didn't think he was doing it all the time. He says he kept it a secret from her and he has been secretly using all these years. That's why he says he was violent. When he got out of jail he put himself in a drug rehabilitation program. He's doing that now. About the day he got so upset he says, "Maybe I did do all of those things, I don't remember. I was on drugs." That's how he talks about it. He also was in the service and got some sort of discharge on a psychological disability. But I haven't found out yet what that was. This man has this history of problems. I have this case and I don't want anyone to get hurt.

HALEY One problem with the case is that I think you don't like the man and you think he's after you. If you think that, that's a real handicap.

GROVE I have a confession to make. I'm seeing this family at a
clinic in southern Ohio. It was hard for me to give him my
card that had my business address on it. I am afraid of him. I
don't mind admitting it.

HALEY It makes you biased in the way you listen to him. If you
set a condition that he meet with the kids and at the end of
the session he says he doesn't want to meet with the kids right
now, I wouldn't take it as you took it, that it was something
about you. I would take it that he doesn't want to see the kids
until he can say something clear about his relationship with his
wife and not with what he and the wife are going to do all
ambiguous.

GROVE I am going to bat for him to have visits with the kids. I
told him, "One thing I will do for you is advocate that you see
your children. I'll put that in writing. Because I think you do
need to see them and they need to see you." He appreciated
that.

HALEY Do you have power to make a decision like that?

GROVE I can recommend that to children's services. They'll listen
to me.

HALEY You've seen the kids separately?

GROVE I saw them all as a group. I spent some time with them
all together and then I saw each one alone. The little boy I
couldn't see alone because he was so upset. I put the 15 year
old in charge of helping him. He and the sister met with me,
and he handled that fine. He says his problem is he misses his
dad. The dad took him to ball games and did all kinds of nice
things with him. Now he doesn't know if he can ever see his
dad again.

HALEY Have you decided whether you would like the couple back
together or separate?

GROVE I wish they'd stay separated. Their problem is that she
keeps these things secret because she's afraid to tell him and

then he knows there's something secret. He then becomes para-
noid. When she finally says whatever it is, he explodes. That's
their pattern. I told them that one goal they needed to have as
a couple is that she can say what's on her mind and he can
hear it and handle it without getting violent.

HALEY You're worried about the possibility that he will not be
able to restrain himself.

GROVE That's right.

HALEY Therefore, somebody else will have to restrain him.

GROVE That's exactly right.

HALEY But he thinks he can restrain himself.

GROVE He thinks he can, yes. He says, "The violence is over. I'll
never hit her again. I was wrong. I was taking drugs and now
I'm not taking drugs anymore." That's his position.

HALEY Is he on a urine test at the rehabilitation?

GROVE I don't know. I need to get information to see what drugs
they found in his system.

HALEY You say that like you don't believe he was on drugs.

GROVE I don't know what to believe. The wife doesn't think he
was on drugs. He says he was and kept it a secret from his wife.
I'm being cautious about it. Maybe I'm being too cautious. I
don't want anyone to get hurt.

HALEY You don't have to take the case.

GROVE Oh God, no. That's why I gave him conditions.

HALEY He knows you don't have to see him?

GROVE I said, "You can work with another therapist if you want.
You don't have to work with me if you don't want. If you
want to work with me, and you want my help getting your
family back together, these are the conditions that I would ask
you to follow. You have to decide whether you can follow
them or not. If you can't, you can see another therapist. You
don't have to see me." Now that's just how I told him.

HALEY   OK. How's he doing on your conditions? Has he turned
the guns in?

GROVE   There's a catch with everything. The wife's living at the
house. The court ordered him to stay away from the house.
That's one reason why he's living with his mother. He says the
guns are at the house, and he's not allowed by the court to go
get them.

HALEY   Why can't the wife turn them in?

GROVE   I didn't think of that. I guess she could do that. That would
be a good one because I think it would be hard for him to
allow her to do that.

HALEY   She'd have to participate in defending herself by getting rid
of them.

GROVE   That's right. Other than the guns, he's following my conditions.

HALEY   Do he and his wife spend the night together?

GROVE   I don't think so. They're doing things like going to AA
meetings together, going to church together, and going to
Bingo together. One demand she has of him if they get back
together is that she's allowed to have friends and leave the
house and do things that she wants to do, like go to church.
That's one of her conditions. He's agreed to that.

HALEY   Before he didn't allow that?

GROVE   No.

HALEY   Was it jealousy?

GROVE   It was serious jealousy, yes. When she was sneaking around
to go grocery shopping, he was assuming that it was another
man that she was seeing. He's jealous and very possessive of
her. He doesn't allow her to have any friends or go anywhere.
It's one of those.

HALEY   But at the moment she's going where she pleases?

GROVE   Only to a point. She does talk to him every single day.
She either talks to him by phone or they see each other.

HALEY   She's certainly not separate then, is she!

GROVE   She doesn't sleep with him, though. He sleeps at his mother's house. She sleeps either at one of her sisters' houses or their house by herself.

HALEY   She doesn't mind being in that house by herself?

GROVE   Apparently not. When I had her mother and the three sisters in, I said to everybody, "I wish that someone would be with her 24 hours a day until or unless he changes and no one's afraid of him." Her mother said, "I'd be glad to do that." But the wife's the one who's not sticking to that. She has every opportunity to have people with her. Her family has agreed to stay with her. But she's not sticking to that. She voluntarily goes and sees him by herself. What I don't know is whether he's pressured her to do that and she's giving in, or whether she really is not afraid of him.

   She says to me that right now she's not afraid of him. I asked her, "Are you going over there because you don't want to have an argument with him or are you really not afraid of him?" She said, "He's treating me pretty well right now. I think he's OK right now."

HALEY   What was the reason he put the gun to his head? What set him off?

GROVE   When he found that she'd left and gone to the shelter. He says he doesn't even remember that. He says he was on drugs that night and the next day. He doesn't remember some of the things he did. He threatened to kill the police officers and he threatened to kill his friend who called the police. I talked to one of the police officers. The police officer himself said, "I'm afraid of this man. I've been on the force for 20 years and I haven't been afraid of anybody. But this man I'm afraid of."

HALEY   If it wasn't for the gun to the head, it would just be a domestic violence case. He beat up his wife and she went to the shelter. But when he barricades himself in an office and holds the police at bay for six hours, that makes it so dramatic.

It's a question of whether he was high, or desperate that one day, or if this is part of his character.

GROVE I'm worried it's part of his character.

HALEY If it's part of his character, you can't trust him to exercise restraint. He might let go at any time; therefore, he has to be monitored from outside. If it's not part of his character, he's learned his lesson now and he won't beat her, he'll behave himself. Because he wants her and the kids back.

GROVE How do you figure out whether it's part of his character or not?

HALEY (*laughs*) That's the problem. I would begin by bringing the couple into sessions and saying that you have grave doubts about whether they should get back together because he was violent before. Apparently he would like it and perhaps she would like it. But you have your doubts. You'd like to have them be able to discuss different issues and you'd like to start with the question of his jealousy. Start with that.

GROVE Not the question about money? That's what they said they fought the most about. You're saying jealousy was in the background of that.

HALEY Right. What was she using the money for and so on. But I would start with jealousy. He might want to start with a smaller problem and work up to it. But I would certainly get to it as soon as you could.

GROVE The jealousy is the central thing.

HALEY This man wants her and doesn't want anybody else to have her, and he's desperate.

GROVE Right. He doesn't have anybody else.

HALEY You could make a condition, too, that he have a job before they go back together. What's she living on now?

GROVE God, I'm not sure. I don't know how she's living. That's a good question. After he lost that job, he got a job in a factory.

He said he was constantly worried about getting injured on that job. He said that made him tense and he would come home in a terrible mood.

HALEY What I worry about is that he's not taking responsibility himself. It's other people. It's the drugs, it's the alcohol. It's something.

GROVE How can I force that issue?

HALEY I would just get him to admit, in her presence, that he did these things. That he's responsible.

GROVE Do you have a way of saying that to a man who was a drug addict so that he has to concede that he was responsible? How do you get him to concede that?

HALEY You have to say, "The only way you can take responsibility for this is never to use drugs again."

GROVE He's already agreed to do that.

HALEY Then I would congratulate him. "That's a responsible position to take." If he becomes violent when intoxicated and he's agreed to stop drinking, that's a responsible thing to do. The question is: Does he have to be monitored? One way to think about it would be to have the judge agree that if he hits her once, or if he has a dirty urine, he'll have to have a court order to keep separate. That way he's monitored by the court and by the drug rehabilitation center.

GROVE For how long a period?

HALEY Whatever the judge would do it for. If he thought he was absolutely going to lose her if he hit her, I don't think he'd hit her. I think he has that much control—if he knows the court would make the separation. I'd have her sign an agreement on that.

GROVE What I'm afraid of is that if he ever hits her and knows he's going to lose her, then he might as well do himself and her in. You wouldn't worry about that possibility?

HALEY You always worry about it. But at the same time, I don't know of another way to stop a man from hitting his wife except to have severe consequences if he does.

GROVE   Right. I need the judge to say, "Either you go to jail or you go to treatment." Then the treatment has the authority to set up conditions.

HALEY   One of the things that often helps is to have the man post a bond, a thousand dollars. If he hits her, she gives the money to her mother. But in this case there's no money, so you can't do that. One thing I would do with this man is to say that he has to go to work before he can go back with his wife. I'd make that one of the conditions. He has to support his wife and kids. One way to do it is to say that, "Because of the way you behaved, for whatever reason, drugs or whatever, people think you're abnormal. They think you're crazy. Because of that you're going to have to live very normally for a period of time before people will begin to accept you."

GROVE   That means taking a job because that's what normal people do.

HALEY   "That means a job. That means supporting your wife and kids. That means not getting drunk or taking drugs. It means being a steady citizen. You'll have to be that way for quite a while before people will believe you. One way to be sure you're that way for quite a while is to have a court order that you're through if you hit her." There are a surprising number of men who won't hit their wives if you set up consequences.

GROVE   I wish you could see the man yourself.

HALEY   (laughs) He's that far out!

GROVE   Here's my physical description for him. He has no fingernails, has shaking hands, and is constantly sweating.

HALEY   Every time you see him?

GROVE   While he's sitting there shaking and sweating, he says, "I'm doing better, my nerves are better now."

HALEY   Where is his father?

GROVE   His father's dead. Why do you ask about his father?

HALEY If a kid is violent you assume two people are in conflict about how to deal with him. One adult is on his side, and one's against him. If an older man is violent, I think there's still two people in conflict about him. One on his side and one against him.

GROVE I think the mother's on his side and the wife's against him.

HALEY I would think the stepfather's against him. How long has the stepfather been around, do you know?

GROVE It's been a while. The stepfather is this kindly, mild-mannered type of person. Somebody has to be for him. I've thought already that his mother is that person. I've thought if his mother would take a stand he might change.

HALEY His mother has to be for him or he wouldn't be so extreme.

GROVE His mother is this soft-spoken, mild-mannered woman, but I don't know a lot about her. When he had the gun to his head that day, the police brought his wife in to try and talk him out of there. They brought his friend over to try and talk him out of there, and they brought his mother over to try and talk him out of there. His mother was worried about her own safety.

HALEY Really?

GROVE She was worried about talking to her own son without getting hurt.

HALEY He must have had some teenage history with her that set him off on this track.

GROVE What would you do about that? Suppose he did.

HALEY I would involve his mother and the stepfather and raise the question, "What do you do about men who beat their wives?" Ask if the stepfather had any experience with this.

GROVE You're going for drawing out their disagreements?

HALEY You can draw out some of their disagreements, yes, but ultimately you want an agreement where they say, "If you hit her, we're through with you."

GROVE What do you mean, "We're through"?

HALEY   They won't see him again. They won't take him in the house.

GROVE   God. If he hits her again and loses her, you wouldn't want his family to be able to take him in and help him back on his feet?

HALEY   If it's important to him that he be involved with his family, then that would be one consequence. You're looking for consequences so he won't hit his wife, or threaten her, or threaten suicide.

GROVE   You think the consequence ought to be no contact with his parents.

HALEY   I would raise this with his mother and his stepfather. Say, "He doesn't seem to be able to control himself at times. Other people are going to have to do it."

GROVE   "Other people are going to have to take a stand with him so he'll stop hitting."

HALEY   Ask them, "What would you come up with that you feel you could do if he ever hit his wife again?"

GROVE   Does it have to be that he never sees them again?

HALEY   No, it doesn't have to be, but that would be a powerful one. If he's home with mother now, then that's where he goes when he's in trouble. He'd either kill himself or go to jail or a hospital.

GROVE   I don't mind the jail or the hospital.

HALEY   I bet not!

GROVE   I don't want to set up a situation where, if he hits her, then he really has lost everybody—his wife, his family, everybody. Then I'm worried he is going to shoot himself. I'm in favor of a consequence but not that he would lose his family.

HALEY   Sure. Well, his mother might come up with one you wouldn't think of like, "I'd keep him in the basement."

GROVE   But I think she's the one who's supporting him—without question.

HALEY I think it may be that she is beaten by the stepfather, or was by the original father.

GROVE I think it was probably the original father.

HALEY If his father were alive, you could give him the task of going to talk to him.

GROVE Would you bring that out with the mother and stepfather and him? Would you ask if she was hit by his father?

HALEY I would bring out that sometimes men hit their wives. Is that an ordinary thing or is that a strange and unusual thing? If they say it's an ordinary thing, you'd say, "Is there anybody you know who did this?"

GROVE You would say it like that?

HALEY Often working-class people think it's OK for the husband to beat his wife. But if they don't think that, they'd say, "My God! That's a horrible thing for a man to do." then you have a better idea that mother might not have been hit. But I'll bet she was hit frequently. If you think of this man as 12 years old, what you would assume is that he might be in league with, or identifying with or behaving like, a father who treated mother badly. He's modeling himself on that father. There's no reason why he can't be doing that when he's 35. I would wonder if his biological father wasn't a pretty violent fellow.

GROVE What would you do with that now? Have the mother say, "That was a terrible thing for me. I don't want to see you doing that"?

HALEY You have a right when you're talking to this man, and helping him get back with his wife, to say, "Your history becomes important, because you've had quite a history of violence. I wonder if anybody in your family has been violent? What about your original father? What was he like?" Then get into it if you want.

GROVE I could raise this with him alone or with his mother and stepfather.

HALEY Or you could do both. See him, hear him out alone about it, and then again with mother and stepfather.

GROVE   His wife told me that his parents beat him terribly when
  he was a boy.

HALEY   I would ask the parents, "Did you have a problem disciplin-
  ing him when he was a boy? Did you have to treat him pretty
  rough to get him straightened out?"

GROVE   What if the parents did beat him?

HALEY   Then you talk with him alone and ask, "Do you think that
  had an effect on you?" I'd say, "Sometimes when kids are
  whipped they whip others. You'd think they'd be kind to others
  after they experience that, but often they're not." I would say,
  "First you've got to have external controls. But we'll begin to
  work on you getting some control of yourself."

GROVE   Apparently when he was booted out of his job for threatening people he was ordered to go to therapy.

HALEY   Who ordered him?

GROVE   He has some sort of disability. He got discharged from the
  service on a psychological disability. That helped him get his
  job. That plays some role here which I'm not sure about.

HALEY   I would certainly find out about that and ask him what he
  thinks about it. Ask him if he thinks he's over that psychological disability.

GROVE   But you think that scenario where his wife came back to
  the session after she left was an example of a pattern they have?

HALEY   It was a portrait of their marriage.

GROVE   She gives and takes.

HALEY   Or she leaves when somebody pushes her away but then
  she comes back. I think that it leaves the man in an uncertain
  state. She says, "I don't want this anymore." But then she comes
  back.

GROVE   She comes back when he's mad.

HALEY   I think there are two things that make violence. One is
  two adults in conflict about it; that is, if you get two parents

to agree about how to handle a violent child, he often stops doing violence. The other thing is a double bind, in which somebody leads you on and then cuts you off, and leads you on and then cuts you off.

GROVE You're saying I have both things going on at once here. I have to intervene in the marriage to block that and I have to intervene with the parents to block that.

HALEY I think so.

GROVE The third agent to add is the court.

HALEY The court becomes your arm of restraint.

GROVE I need to make a list of things that I need from the judge and send the judge a letter.

HALEY First I think you need to work it out with him, and with her. With him you can have a contract where he'll be restrained for now, but ultimately he's got to restrain himself. Then get the court to restrain him. Work the plan out with him, and then get the court to back you up. That's the way I'd make it.

GROVE What conditions would you want with her?

HALEY I would get her to agree, and maybe sign a document that if he hit her she'd leave. She wouldn't come back like she has before.

GROVE Also that she'd turn the guns in.

HALEY Get rid of the guns, right. You know, what I am suspecting, you absolutely can't trust him, but I think the man may be past this. I think the man may have had time to think about this.

GROVE I've had that thought. He's been out of jail a while now, and if the man was so out of his mind he would have done something by now.

HALEY It's possible that he could be past doing anything else really insane, and therefore the authorities can back off of him. But the problem is, you can't do it halfway. You've either got to have him under the control of the court or let him restrain himself on his own. I'm not saying you should do this. I'm saying the way you describe the situation, it sounds like he may be past this. He's been out of jail. He sees her alone. She's available if he wants to harm her. He's concerned about his kids, but hesitates to see them under these conditions. If he's taken that boy fishing and such, a good part of his life revolves around those kids.

GROVE   He spends a lot of time with his boy. Suppose you're right. He's past it. What would be the consequences of setting it up with the arm of the law restraining him?

HALEY   You don't want to make him not past it by the actions you take to protect her.

GROVE   The consequences would be that it continues to keep the community and her worried about him. That could provoke him?

HALEY   It means every morning when he wakes up he's thinking he's stuck with a court order on his back.

GROVE   The things that I have to do are: getting him and his parents together and having a discussion about getting the mother to take a position.

HALEY   I would talk to him about his natural father. There must be somebody in his family who behaved similarly.

GROVE   If the dad did lose control and hit people, what should I say to the man?

HALEY   I would just tell him that he has to exercise more restraint because hitting runs in his family. He must have had some admiration for that father doing that. It's a way of giving him an excuse for his violent behavior that comes from you, not from him. He says, "It was drugs, and it was drink." You say it's his family. But it's still an excuse for him behaving that way. He must be puzzled about, "What the hell is the matter with me that I would threaten my wife with a gun like that?"

Soon after this consultation the court allowed the children to return to the mother with the man only allowed to visit the family under court supervision. The man then had to face domestic violence charges in court as a result of the abuse towards his wife. Before his court date I explained to the man that if he would agree to several stipulations, I would talk with the judge and recommend that he be ordered into therapy instead of going to jail. My stipulations were that he continue to follow my four conditions and that, in addition to him having to go to jail if he ever hits his wife again, he submit to random drug testing, with the understanding that if he moved back with his wife and a drug test were positive, he would have to move out again until his system as drug-free. He agreed to this plan. I then called the judge and explained that for me to be helpful in this situation I would need the authority of the court behind me. I recommended the man be ordered into therapy and to comply with all of the conditions that I had laid out to him. The judge followed all of my recommendations and the man became much more cooperative with therapy. After his court date he turned in all of his guns to the police. He also found a job which he liked. This helped him immensely.

With the couple, I focused on the man's jealousy. I asked both the husband and the wife what they felt the other did not understand about them. The husband said his wife did not understand how much he really loved her and how much she meant to him. The wife then said that even while they were separated she felt she could not do a thing without her husband knowing exactly where she was or whom she was with. Throughout their marriage the husband monitored his wife constantly. He felt she was the only person in the world for him and he was desperate to not let anyone else around her.

I framed the problem as the husband having too much love for his wife. This was making him insanely jealous. He would have to learn to tolerate her having some distance from him. I asked the wife to make a list of things she would like the freedom to do without her husband monitoring her. She said, "I would like to take a walk for 15 minutes and not have to be afraid of how he'll react. I would like to talk to someone in public once in a while and not be interrogated later about who that person was."

The wife made her list and the couple began to practice having the wife do more and more without the husband knowing what she was doing. The husband was able to tolerate his wife having more distance and the mood between the couple improved. The wife also signed in front of her husband a document which I prepared stating that if they got back together and he ever hit her she would divorce him. This simple procedure had a powerful impact on the couple.

I then saw the husband alone and asked why he was discharged from the military. He was discharged from the service 17 years prior to the therapy. He told an incredible, complicated story about how he was stationed on a ship and continuously harassed by a fellow serviceman. He said the man harassed him daily and he, my client, "lost it." He brutally killed the man with a baseball bat. He said, "I bashed him until his head caved in."

He was diagnosed as mentally ill and discharged. I was stunned by the gruesome details of his story. He said I was the first person he had told this story to. He had not told anyone in his family, nor had he ever told his wife. In this session he said he continued to have violent nightmares and was preoccupied with suicide. He said it was good that I had him turn his guns in because he might have shot himself with one of them. I was very disturbed by this new information and decided to enlist his family to help him over his suicidal ideation.

I invited his parents to join him for the next session. His mother said she could not explain why her son was so violent. I asked her if my client had given her serious trouble while growing up and if they ever had to hit him to correct him. The mother said he never gave them any serious trouble and they never had to hit him. I asked if anyone else in the family had any trouble with being violent. The parents said no one in the family was violent. His real father, who was now deceased, never hit his mother and her current husband never hit her. She said the one problem she had with her son was that for the past several years he had withdrawn from the family.

She wished he would confide in her more about his problems and keep in closer touch with her. I then had the mother move closer to her son and take his hand, look him in the eyes and say to him that she loved him and did not want him to kill himself. The mother was very sincere in repeating this to her son. She spontaneously added that even if he and his wife did break up she would want him to handle that. She said, "It was hard for me to lose my husband, but I got through that." The man was moved by his mother's words.

For the next session I invited the couple and their three children. After discussing several family issues, I had each child sit next to the father and tell him they loved him and did not want him to kill himself. This was very powerful for the children. When I first began to work with the family, the children had all expressed concern that their father might shoot himself. The son wanted to repeat his turn several times. He then began to cry and told his father, "Don't shoot mom." The father was very moved by his children.

At the end of this session I explained to the man alone that I had given a lot of thought to the story he told about killing a man. I explained that I thought it was imperative that he tell his wife this story. He was very much against telling his wife. I told him that he could not keep something like that a secret from his wife. If he did he would always be doubting in his mind if she would really accept him if she knew the truth about his past. Although he objected strongly, he did tell his wife.

In the next session I saw the wife alone. She said her husband had told her the exact story he had told me. She explained that despite his violent past she was feeling much better about him. Since he had been out of jail he had not hit her or threatened her verbally or even given her an intimidating look. He was allowing her the freedoms she had asked for on her list and was ready for him to come home.

I then got the couple together and said that, although I was very glad things were improving between them, I had serious doubts about their getting back together. I explained that if they both wanted back together I would continue to work with them, but things would have to be very different from before.

Two Months Later

GROVE The general situation is that the husband is cooperating with everything I'm asking of him. He's much improved and he's treating his wife much better. He's worked hard on his jealousy. He's now letting his wife walk around the block without interrogating her. The wife told me alone that she feels much better about him and wants him to come home. I'm to the point where they've done everything I can think of while they're separated and if she now wants him back I'm going to have to back off and let them get back together.

HALEY Has the wife ever said in this man's presence that she will never have an affair?

GROVE No.

HALEY If he's agreed to not be jealous and allow her to go places, then I think she should agree not to have an affair.

GROVE That's a good idea. I've been thinking about making a contract where if they get back together and she becomes afraid of him then he'll have to go to his mother's. He'll have to leave. They have had a pattern where she leaves him and then goes back to him. You were right. That has been a portrait of their marriage. The pattern was that she would leave and go to her mother's. She would stay there overnight and then go back home. A month later they'd have a fight again and she'd go back to her mother's. I'm thinking about having them change that pattern so that *he* has to leave if she becomes afraid—not if he hits her, but if she just becomes afraid and worried he might hit her—then he has to go to his mother's.

HALEY Another way to go would be to have her go somewhere else besides her mother's.

GROVE Change where she goes rather than who goes.

HALEY One thing I've done is to get an agreement from the wife that if she leaves, she goes to a hotel. She won't want to go to a hotel and he won't want her to go to a hotel so they don't escalate to the point where that happens.

GROVE   Do you think it would have the same effect if he has to go to his mother's? I want to stop their cycle.

HALEY   I think that would be fine. The case I'm thinking of is a woman who'd escalate a fight with her husband, then go away to her family. It began to be clear that every time there was a holiday she had a fight with her husband so she had to go to her family's.

GROVE   OK.

HALEY   We just told her she couldn't go to the family if she had a fight with her husband and that stopped the fighting. If she had a fight she had to go to a hotel instead.

GROVE   Was her husband a jealous, violent man?

HALEY   Not really, no. He was a nice man. But she had a problem with her family, she couldn't just go visit them. She had to be fleeing from something in order to visit.

GROVE   Was it that they didn't want to see her unless she had a problem?

HALEY   I think it was partly that, yes. But it made me realize that you can stop the escalation of the fights by changing the way the fights end.

GROVE   OK. With my couple, what other agreements do you think I need?

HALEY   I would meet with them and say that you've advised them to separate and they don't seem to be going to do that. You can say you considered just insisting on their separating and you realized they wouldn't separate. They want to be together. Therefore, if they're going to be together they have to be together on terms where what happened in the past never happens again. You would like them to have an agreement that he won't threaten her in any way. She won't make him jealous in any way, or have an affair with anyone else. I'm thinking she must lead him on, you know. Then I would set this up by asking them to have a three-month trial in which they live together. If they have any difficulty during that period, then at the end of three months they'll split.

GROVE They'll get a divorce.

HALEY Right.

GROVE That's a good idea. Set up a three-month trial. Then they'll probably not have any problems for three months.

HALEY I think not. Then at the end of three months you can renew it for another three months.

GROVE Go one step at a time. That's a very good way of doing it. I have everything in place that we discussed the last time except for his mother having a consequence for if he hits his wife again. I am really hesitant about having his mother disowning him over that. I told his mother, "I need you to help me take a stand with him against violence." I said, "Can you put your mind to this?" I knew I had to give her examples of what she might do, but I didn't have any examples. I just wanted to raise the idea in a general way first, with the agreement that she'll come back again to settle this. I have her thinking about what stance she wants to take. She called me up later and said, "I enjoyed that session and I'll come back again if you want."

HALEY She must be desperate. The poor lady. With a son like that.

GROVE She's so worried about him. She has poor health, too. He doesn't want to come to her with his problems because he's worried it's a burden on her.

HALEY Sure. You know one function of his extreme behavior may be to hold his mother up in some way, or to give her some purpose in life.

GROVE If he's helping her it must have started because she had a hard time after she lost her husband.

HALEY I just wonder if when she gets depressed, he makes trouble or frightens her. If he does something to pull her out of her depression.

GROVE   Why should she say she didn't have any trouble out of him when he was a child? She put it as though he has withdrawn from her and is closemouthed about his problems with her. She's upset about that. She wants to know what is going on with him.

HALEY   Maybe it's true that how he's behaving has nothing to do with his mother, but often if you have a man behaving so extremely he's protecting someone.

GROVE   Suppose he is protecting her—then what?

HALEY   In this three-month trial period I would just try to think of getting his mother involved with him in some way. Once a week they can go have dinner with her.

GROVE   I could suggest that they invite her over, because his wife complains that his mother hasn't paid much attention to her kids.

HALEY   You'd have to give a reason, like his mother needs to be reassured that they're getting along all right during this three-month period. Therefore, they should have her over every week.

GROVE   I think that's a very good idea.

HALEY   That would help just in case his behavior has some function with helping his mother. He could check on her every week or two without making trouble.

GROVE   That would be such a change for this couple. They never had his mother over for dinner. I think that's a good idea. It's just one more thing that is very different from how they were before.

HALEY   You could say that, compared to the way it was before, they need to change the way they get along with each other and with other people. They've got to do things differently now and this would be one thing different.

GROVE   I know he'd go along with that because he wants his mother to be reassured about how he is doing. Do you have any other ideas on his mother besides the couple having her over for dinner?

HALEY   Not that I can think of right off. Have they ever taken a
   vacation?

GROVE   I don't know. I realized when they were talking about his
   jealousy that he doesn't know how to please her. He doesn't
   know how to do something romantic with her so that she's
   really pleased and he can see that he's pleased her. If he could
   do that then I think he would be reassured that she really
   wants to be with him. Then he might not get so jealous. I told
   him, "I wish that you would do something romantic with your
   wife." He said something in a dejected way about how he
   doesn't know how to romance her. I think that's very crucial.
   Instead of romancing her and pleasing her as a way to hold on
   to her, he hits her and threatens her. Then, because he mistreats
   her, he worries that she'll leave him.

HALEY   He must feel she loses interest in him and then when he
   hits her she gets involved with him again.

GROVE   Yes.

HALEY   One thing to do would be to say that another requirement
   of the three-month trial period is that at the end of it they
   have to go away for the weekend together, without the kids.
   They could go somewhere which he chooses that he knows
   she would like. He'll spend three months trying to figure out
   what she might like.

GROVE   That's a nice idea. That weekend has to be the time of her
   life.

HALEY   His mother could take care of the kids while they're gone.
   It doesn't have to be too expensive. They could go to West
   Virginia and stay in a hotel overnight.

GROVE   They could rent a cabin.

HALEY   Sure. It should be something she would like, preferably
   where there's some dancing and music.

GROVE   I wish he'd take dancing lessons with her. That doesn't cost
   a lot of money.

HALEY   I'm sure he's scared that he doesn't know how to dance and that's why he won't do it.

GROVE   Right. So he should just take dancing lessons. They could do that together. He might actually enjoy it.

HALEY   He could do the shake. (*laughs*)

GROVE   (*laughs*) Right. He could just do that naturally. His shaking and sweating are now gone by the way. He is much more relaxed. He's made a lot of very significant changes and he's more relaxed, but he isn't at home. That's what bothers me. He's relaxed while not living with his wife.

HALEY   He's relaxed while he's at his mother's.

GROVE   That's right. He's relaxed at his mother's. I think that's a good idea to have the mother go over there every week. That does sound like he's worried about his mother, doesn't it?

HALEY   It sounds like it.

GROVE   The only thing that does still concern me about this man is that every once in a while he still lapses into saying these very extreme things. For example, the court took away all of his guns for one year. He said, "I better have them back before that." Then he said, "Do you know how easy it would be to kill someone? If I wanted to kill you, all I'd have to do is rig your car so that when you turned it on, the car would blow up. There'd be no evidence." He said this to me.

HALEY   How did you respond?

GROVE   I said, "I hope you don't do anything like that!" Then I said, "I know you're mad at me because I asked you to give up your guns. My criterion for your having your guns back is that nobody in your house is nervous about your having them. If everybody is comfortable with your having them, then I'm not going to make an issue out of it."

HALEY   When he says something extreme, I think the way to answer that is to tell him he has to stop that. If he says, "Stop what?" then you say, "Stop saying exaggerated threats that worry people and get you into such trouble. You shouldn't say anything like blowing up somebody's car. Never say that again."

GROVE Handle it like a psychotic person, like he might be uncertain of how he comes across?

HALEY Handle it like a man who doesn't realize that he scares people by telling these stories, right. Tell him he should stop bringing them up.

GROVE Give him the benefit of the doubt that he isn't doing it on purpose. What if he doesn't stop it?

HALEY What I'm thinking of is when he makes a threat like that and you say, "I hope you don't do that." I don't think that's as good as your responding at the level of his threat. You have to say something stronger like, "You better cut these threats out."

GROVE I have to respond at the same level of his extreme statements.

HALEY Right.

GROVE I'm sure he'll give me another opportunity.

HALEY He may say, "I wasn't threatening," and so on. Then you say, "Well, then you better think about how you talk because it sounds like you're threatening and you have to stop that."

GROVE What if he says, "What if I don't stop it? What will you do if I say it again?"

HALEY I don't think he would do that. I think it would surprise him that you would say he shouldn't talk like that. I don't think anybody's ever told him he shouldn't talk like that. No one has ever said, "You have to stop that."

GROVE What if he does say, "What will you do about it?" and makes it into a macho thing?

HALEY I don't think he would. But if he did, you could say, "I'm not going to do anything about it, but you better do something about it because you're going to end up in trouble all over again."

GROVE   "This is what you lost your wife over."

HALEY   That's right. Ask him, "What do you gain by threatening people?"

GROVE   I just can't believe I've gotten as far as I have with this man.

HALEY   It's remarkable.

GROVE   I'm thinking that I will be involved with this couple for a while.

HALEY   At some point you shouldn't have to be seeing them every week. But you should be seeing them occasionally and be in their life as a monitor for quite a while.

GROVE   Yes. But at what point do I begin to back off?

HALEY   Once this man can monitor his own violent behavior you're through.

GROVE   Right. The question is: When do I know that he's monitoring himself? What kind of things would you look for on that?

HALEY   If he can have a period of time in which he makes no threats to himself or others and if he survives some crisis with his wife without getting violent.

GROVE   When they get a huge bill and he can handle that without getting violent.

HALEY   Who pays the bills, do you know?

GROVE   She would present him with the bills and he would pay them. That was another one of the changes she wanted in order for her to take him back.

HALEY   You could just set it up that, since money was an issue between them, you'd like one of them to handle the bills and the money and you'd prefer it was her. Let her pay all of the bills.

GROVE   Once they get back together, I'm assuming that several issues will come up that haven't come up so far, since they haven't been living together.

HALEY   Sure. You can anticipate those with them. What if the
electricity bill goes too high? What if when she goes to the
store she comes home later than he thinks she should.

GROVE   I can have a discussion like that with them before they get
back together.

HALEY   Then, when some of these things come up, there's at least
a little preparation. I definitely think you should do something
about how they are handling the bills. If she gives him a bill
and he has to pay it, then he might protest that it's too high
and blame her. She may not have been the one to run up the
electricity. If it's the other way around, if he gives her the bill
and she has to pay it, then she could protest.

GROVE   He's saying he protested because he wanted that money to
buy drugs.

HALEY   You can tell him he doesn't need that anymore but still he
needs this change. It reminds me of a case we had where the
husband was a golf addict. He didn't work but he insisted on
paying the bills. The wife gave him the money and then he
didn't pay the bills. He used it for golf. Her parents were
visiting and the water was turned off because he hadn't paid
the bill.

Follow-Up

Soon after this consultation I organized a meeting with several professionals who were working with this man. The meeting included
myself, the man's drug counselor, his probation officer, and a psychologist whom the court had hired to do testing on him. Everyone
at this meeting agreed that the man had improved significantly. The
psychologist, who had stretched his testing out over a long period of
time, said he had never seen a man like this make such a dramatic
improvement in such a short time. Everyone agreed it was time to
allow the man to move back home.

I followed Haley's suggestion and set up a three-month trial period with the couple. The agreement was that if the man hit his wife, they were through. To improve the romantic feelings between him and his wife, during this period, the man followed several suggestions and initiated some ideas of his own. He arranged for a weekend away with just his wife. The couple greatly enjoyed this.

One major issue turned out to be very serious conflict between the man's mother and his wife. My initial intuition about the family was correct. The hottest triangle was the man, his mother, and his wife. This became apparent when I suggested that the couple invite the man's mother to their home for dinner. The wife became very upset by this idea and refused. I met alone with the man's mother and his wife and emphasized that I was very concerned that the man would not react well to continued tension between the two of them. I stressed the need for a truce. They agreed to at least be civil with each other. They seemed to find a way to get along after a family cook-out at the man's mother's home, which the wife attended.

A second major issue concerned the man's persistence in saying things that implied he might become violent, which frightened people. Although he was not saying these statements to his wife, he was saying them to me and other professionals. I realized that all during the therapy the man had responded when I got tough with him. I had a very frank and very tough talk with him, insisting that he completely cut out such talk. Amazingly, the man responded and stopped using any scary language.

Throughout therapy, I met periodically with the wife alone to check with her about the man's behavior and to make sure she felt safe being around him. After the three-month trial period had ended, the wife told me that she continued to feel safe around him. She said, "I can disagree with him now without being afraid he might hurt me." To my knowledge, since the beginning of the therapy to the present, a period of nine months, the man has not hit his wife, threatened her verbally, or given her an intimidating look, or threatened her with gestures.

I am continuing to meet periodically with this couple and plan to stay involved for quite a while.

4 | INFIDELITY

THE LOST ARTIST

GROVE This is a young couple in their early thirties, with no children. It's a couple where the husband is really lost.

HALEY She's bringing him in saying, "Do something about him!"?

GROVE It's worse than that, but that's basically it. She sent him in. Let me tell you about these two. When they got married they were both musicians and earning no money. She came from a proper Catholic family. He doesn't come from a religious family. Somewhere along the line, she decided to be realistic. She got a computer programming degree. She is now a computer programmer and a very together woman. He's a vacuum cleaner salesman, and a lost soul. Recently, the husband had a sexual encounter with a teenage girl. The wife found out about it and separated from him. That's when he came to me. At the time both he and this girl had night jobs at the same company. He ended up having sex with her in the office at night.

The girl tried to call the husband at his home and the wife answered the phone. When the wife confronted the husband he confessed to her about the sex. She then moved out of the house and was going to divorce him. She had made up her mind, but she talked to her priest and her priest persuaded her to not act so quickly. She started having second thoughts and

told him, "Maybe I'll stay, if you shape up." One of her require-
ments was that he get therapy. He then came in and saw me
the first time alone. Now he's trying to do all sorts of things to
reform himself in order to win her back. He's holding onto his
vacuum cleaner salesman job, he's joining the Catholic Church,
and he's seeing me as ordered.

HALEY   He's a vacuum cleaner salesman?

GROVE   He's a vacuum cleaner salesman. It's a shaky job. She has
her computer programming job, is in control of all the money,
and does everything that you're supposed to do. He, on the
other hand, has his shaky job, goes behind her back, lies, and
had sex with a teenage girl.

HALEY   I get the picture.

GROVE   You got the picture. I saw him alone once. Then I called
her up and had her come in alone. She basically has one foot
in the marriage and one foot out. She said she still loves him
and doesn't want to divorce him, but she doesn't want to get
close to him either. She's moved into her own apartment.

   After struggling and pulling teeth, I got the wife to come in
with the husband. I tried to set up a therapy framework where
she would set a date to decide what she would do about her
marriage. She rejected that all together. Even that is farther
than she wanted to go with him. Right now they're just having
breakfast together, occasionally. That's all that she'll do.

HALEY   How do they get together for breakfast?

GROVE   He calls her up and invites her out to breakfast. She won't
date him. I told him, "Look, you have to see her. You want to
win your wife back, you have to see her. So call her up, see if
she'll have breakfast with you."

HALEY   She's not up to having dinner with him?

GROVE   She's not up to having dinner. I said, "Don't call it a date,
just ask her to meet you for a cup of coffee and see if she'll
have breakfast with you." She's doing that. When I see him
alone I'm coaching him on how to deal with her. When I saw

her alone, she said she still loves him but she just doesn't know if she could trust him again. I'm thinking I need an ordeal for them to get over the past.

HALEY   Sure.

GROVE   But I think the larger problem, which I wanted to talk to you about, is that he is so down in relation to her. I mean, she outdoes him in every area of their life together. I think the problem is more than that affair. She said, "I'm humiliated. I'm so humiliated. I want to be proud of what he's doing." She said that in relation to the affair, but I heard that in relation to everything. The problem is, how to get this guy more respectable.

HALEY   Does he have any interests in anything, like art or sculpting?

GROVE   Well, he's interested in music. They were musicians.

HALEY   Does he have an instrument?

GROVE   Yes, but I don't know what it is. I didn't ask him what he plays.

HALEY   Do you know if he composes?

GROVE   I don't know, but that's a good idea. He's an artist. That's what you're going for.

HALEY   Right.

GROVE   Artists are not supposed to be good in the real world. They're artists.

HALEY   They have the prestige that comes from being an artist.

GROVE   Yes.

HALEY   From being the way he is.

GROVE   Yes! That's a good way.

HALEY   If he could get even a minor job in some music field, it would be so much better than selling, which he's probably not so great at.

GROVE   Or if he sold something, it would be to support his real talent.

HALEY Right. Maybe, if he is a composer, which he might be, he could say that he would like to have three months without working, just to compose. She would have to support him while he's composing. Right now, are they blending money?

GROVE Yes. They still have joint accounts. The main problem is how to help her past this humiliation. I thought of sending him to a priest for an ordeal but I don't know if that's going to be strong enough for her. It has to be something humiliating for him. I should talk to him alone about that.

HALEY I would ask her what he could do that would make up to her for the terrible thing he did.

GROVE I asked her, in his presence, and she said she couldn't think of anything. You think I should ask again with her alone?

HALEY I think you have to give her examples.

GROVE Say some things that you've done on that. There's no money, so I don't think he can give her money.

HALEY Does the man have a problem with her mother?

GROVE Her mother? No, he and her mother get along. But he and her sister don't get along, if you're looking for someone he doesn't get along with.

HALEY He could do something humiliating, in relation to a relative of hers. I was thinking, if he took his mother-in-law on a cruise . . . (*laughter*)

GROVE In fact, he went and visited her mother after this all happened. He called up her mother and said, "Can I come over and talk to you?" Her mother is really fond of him. As a way to help himself win his wife back, he's trying to make an alliance with her mother.

HALEY The bad feeling is between him and her sister?

GROVE Yes. You think that if this man did something humiliating in relation to his sister-in-law that might be sufficient?

HALEY He could do something positive for the sister-in-law.

GROVE   He could sell her a vacuum cleaner and not take his commission.

HALEY   Some special vacuum cleaner. But it would be better if he'd
take the mother on a cruise.

GROVE   They like each other already so that wouldn't have the
meaning you're after. In general, though, I hadn't thought
about him doing something for her family. I think that helping
her sister would be good because the husband would hate that
and that would show his wife that he really is serious about
wanting to reform himself.

HALEY   If you got her interested in that as a solution, then if he
did it, she'd have to go back to him. One of the reasons for
having a penance is that once the villain does it, the other spouse
is obligated. They can't just say, "Well, that's not enough, I still
don't want to go back."

GROVE   His penance could either be something with her sister or
something that she would be proud of him for doing that he
wouldn't ordinarily do. Because she said she's ashamed of him.
He could volunteer for the poor, or something like that. Because she's humiliated. What struck me is that she said, "I'm
humiliated, I want to be proud of him." He could do something
that she'd be proud of, so that she could say to her family,
"Look what he did." He has to do something to help her past
her humiliation.

HALEY   He has to be redefined in some way for her to be accepting
of him.

GROVE   That's how you're proposing to help him out of being
one-down. To try and redefine him in some way, without him
having to change jobs, or careers, or go back to school, or
something like that.

HALEY   Anything that would take time like that is a problem.

GROVE   Although he should do something like that anyway. You
know, it's hard for me because I'm not seeing him in a very

positive light. Although I like him. I can see that he is just so lost. I don't see anything in him that I can say with my heart, "Look, he's this!"

HALEY But you have to keep in mind, she chose him. So, she must have wanted him.

GROVE Well, she chose him at a time when she was interested in artistic things. But now she's moved to a different lifestyle, and he's struggling to change with her. She rejected the artist life-style and him too. That's what I'm worried is going on.

HALEY Well, he should go back into that lifestyle.

GROVE You think he should go back into that lifestyle rather than join her in hers.

HALEY From the way you describe him, he's not going to make it in hers, I don't think.

GROVE No, he isn't.

HALEY I mean, if he were a super salesman, making lot of money, then he might. But he must have given up his artistic lifestyle partly to please her.

GROVE Yes, I think he did.

HALEY If he could be involved in music, and if when he was supposed to see her he had a commitment in relation to music and preferred that instead, it would be a great step forward for him, you know?

GROVE That's a great idea. It would make him more interesting to her. It might make him more desirable to her.

HALEY I think the best way to raise a man in relation to a woman is to make him unpredictable, doing things that she wouldn't anticipate. Because she thinks she has him figured out now.

GROVE That's right.

HALEY What would really make a change would be if you could get him interested in art again, so if you had a session with them together and she wanted something from him you could say to her, "Well, you can't expect that with an artist you know."

GROVE   Yes.

HALEY   In a powerful way, that can work out. Sometimes you can do it with adolescents.

GROVE   I could do it with him now, and say, "The problem is that you're an artist at heart, struggling to be in the real world. You're a lost soul in the real world."

HALEY   Trying to be a yuppie.

GROVE   That's right! He's an artist trying to be a yuppie. That's a good way of putting it. The problem is, he has to go back to being an artist. Then he'll have more confidence, he'll get his soul back.

HALEY   That's right. Or he has to manage somehow to make it in the yuppie world, even if he is an artist. To make use of his talents some way.

Follow-Up

This couple was a testimonial to the power of reframing. After this consultation I saw them one more time. The wife at that point was clearly more concerned about "being proud of her husband in general" than she was resentful about the affair. I therefore concentrated on reframing the husband with the purpose of raising his status. It turned out that he was an excellent musician before they were married. He performed in a string quartet and he had students whom he instructed. He gave all of that up after he got married, thinking that he would have to take on the responsibility of providing for a family, and that as a musician he would not be able to do that.

I gave a speech to him and his wife about how he was a true artist at heart and that without his music he was a lost soul. Both husband and wife loved this. When I said that, the man sat up in his chair, puffed his chest out, and began to boast of his accomplishments as a musician. The wife talked about how the man she married was a musician and that since he had put up his cello he was not the same person she was proud of. I pushed for him to make music a central part of his life again. The couple proceeded to have a 45-minute conversation about how he could take on some students again, and how he could get back in the quartet. The session ended with the husband asserting himself and planning how he could again be a musician. The wife was very pleased.

After this session, I did not hear from this couple for several months, so I called them to follow up. I spoke with the wife. She said that she had moved back in with him shortly after their last session with me, and that she felt things had improved. The husband was playing his cello again and wanted to take on some students but had not yet done so. I did not hear from them after that, and I assume they are doing fine.

Discussion

This case is a classic example of a situation which I believe to be more and more common in marital therapy. A wife is faced with a husband who is struggling in some way, and she has been trying on her own to help him. This is a next to impossible situation for her, because even if her husband ends up making changes, he is not the one initiating the changes. He is changing only because she is arranging for him to. The couple can easily end up in a pattern where the wife initiates everything and the husband only responds to what the wife initiates. He does not assert himself. This is often unsatisfying to the wife, who wants her husband to make a change that comes from his heart.

Many times, as with this particular couple, the wife has to resort to bringing her husband to a therapist, whom she wants to take over and reform her husband. The husband in such situations can often be in pretty bad shape and the wife may be expressing ambivalence about staying with him. I believe, however, that it is a serious error to encourage a split, even if the husband does appear to have terrible problems. It is better to assume that the wife really wants the husband to improve himself and that, if he can do this, his wife will happily stay with him.

One way for the therapy to succeed is to find some way to raise the husband's status in the eyes of the wife. This often means arranging some way for the husband to assert himself and initiate something positive on his own. This can be done in several ways. The husband can be put in charge of solving some problem; if he succeeds, his self-esteem will improve. Another way to raise a husband's status is to help him be less predictable and more mysterious. His wife may then find him more interesting and attractive. In the case presented here, this would have been inappropriate, since one of the problems was the husband's secretive behavior. A third way to raise a husband's status, which was used here, is to reframe him in some more positive way. If the wife can accept the reframing and see her husband in a more positive light, the husband can find new ways to assert himself and the wife will end up pleased.

SCHEDULING AFFAIRS

GROVE   I've got a new couple to talk to you about. I don't think this is a particularly hard couple, but it's one where the husband is the one who is presenting the problem, so I thought it would be interesting to talk about.

The spouses are both in their early forties; they have two boys, ages 9 and 12. They've been married about 13 years and it's the only marriage for both of them. They both have college degrees and have professional careers. The husband called me up originally, saying he wanted to come in for therapy because he had a problem. The problem is that he keeps having affairs.

He had been secretly having an affair with another married woman for about one year. Recently his wife found a hotel receipt that the husband could not explain. He then opened up and told his wife about his affair. The next day he called me up wanting to come in and get help. He was desperate to come in, worrying that his wife was going to leave him. I saw him one time, then I saw her one time, and then they both came in together.

When I saw him alone, he told me that he had had three long affairs during the course of their marriage. During his second affair he separated from his wife and then he eventually decided to go back to her. He thinks his wife only knows about the most recent affair. But it turns out that she has suspicions about the others. He just hasn't admitted them to her. She confronted him about her suspicions, but he didn't acknowledge to her that he had had the other affairs.

He's desperate now to save the marriage. When the wife came alone, she said she doesn't know what she wants to do. I think she wants to stay with him, but she just doesn't know how she can trust him again after this. She's struggling with that. When alone with me the husband said that his wife neglects him. They have a sexual relationship, but his biggest complaint about her is that she's compulsive. She works all the time and everything has to be perfect. When they do make love, he has to tear her away from work, which she brings home at night. They go upstairs, they have sex, and then she goes back downstairs and finishes her work.

He, on the other hand, has these girlfriends whom he takes dancing and skiing, and so on. He does these wonderful things with these girlfriends. His wife won't do any of them with him. That's his complaint. Her complaint is that he mistreats her and criticizes her about silly things like how she brushes her teeth.

She says she's afraid because she doesn't know how to read him. This affair took her by surprise. She said, "We've been having a sexual relationship, and I couldn't tell there was any-thing different." While he was having his affair, she thought they had problems, but not to the degree that he would have an affair.

HALEY   What happened when they came in together?

GROVE   When they were together in my office, it looked to me like he couldn't handle her interpersonally. I don't know if he acted that way because right now he has his tail between his legs over this affair or if what I saw represents a long-standing pattern between them. What was happening was that she would start to get angry and talk and talk and talk. He would sit there disagreeing, but he couldn't say anything. He doesn't know how to assert himself with her. If they have a disagreement, she dominates him. About halfway through the session with the two of them, something upset him, and he said, "I don't know about this. This counseling is too one-sided." I didn't know what upset him and I sensed he was not going to say what it was in her presence, so I had her leave the room and I asked him, "What did you mean by that?"

HALEY   What did he mean by that?

GROVE   He thought I was siding with her because I was letting her talk so much. What was important was that she was giving this litany of complaints, and he could not defend himself, even when I asked him, "What's your side of these things?" In her presence he couldn't defend himself. I think he's afraid of her.

HALEY   Is he that one-down because of the affair, is that it?

GROVE   That's what I was trying to figure out. Is he one-down because of the affair or is that a general pattern in their relationship? They both say that over the years there have been some topics they can disagree about and they can resolve. But free time and how to organize the house are two things that they haven't been able to talk about. If they fight about those things, she gets more and more upset. At some point, she gets so upset he says, "My God! Just calm down." It gets to a point where he can't tolerate her being so mad so he backs off, and then nothing gets resolved.

   I'm thinking about a strategy to help these two, but I haven't decided what to do. Since she said she's not sure if she wants to stay with him, I had them set a date by which she should decide. Other than that I have not set up anything. With him having these three affairs and going out and having fun all of the time, I originally thought this was a pattern with him irresponsible and her responsible. I was going to do something around secrets, because he had these secret affairs. I was thinking about her having some secret. But then when I saw them together, I wasn't sure that would be appropriate.

HALEY If the man's already one-down, that could only make it worse.

GROVE Right, that's what's confusing. He acts like she neglects him, and she acts like there's too much on her shoulders. She says she's doing too much, and "By God, if I have to work and come home and do everything at home, I'm not going to spend any time with you." Then he's acting like, "Well, if you're not going to spend any time with me, I'm going to go out and find somebody else."

HALEY Would you like to be reckless?

GROVE How so?

HALEY If you want, you can see them together and say that there's all kinds of ways to be married. If she was surprised by this affair, then she must have thought things were all right while he was having this affair.

GROVE That's what she said.

HALEY So, you ask them what she would think about allowing affairs, since things are all right when he has an affair. Say that affairs seem to stabilize them. Say that with some couples it's all right if the husband has a mistress. With other couples it's a terrible thing.

GROVE Should she be allowed to have an affair, too, then?

HALEY No, I wouldn't say that. I would just ask her what the possibility is that she would just accept his having a woman on the side. Then they wouldn't have to quarrel about it. It would just be part of their arrangement.

GROVE   She wouldn't have to be constantly wondering about it. She would know what's really happening.

HALEY   It could even be scheduled for one day a week. He could have an agreed-upon night out.[1]

GROVE   Why does that fit with this couple?

HALEY   Well, because it's true. He's had a series of affairs, and it's seemed to stabilize them. If she's a woman who'll rush upstairs to have sex, and then rush back downstairs to go to work, she really doesn't want to be bothered with that side of her life.

GROVE   Do you think I should talk to her alone about it, or should I do it with both of them?

HALEY   If you do it with her alone, then you're making a more serious proposal that she should do this. What you want is to have them together, and you propose this, and then the husband will give you a stout denial of wanting that. He'll say he doesn't want that kind of marriage.

GROVE   She'll say that too. I understand. You want them to abandon their pattern. That's what you're after.

HALEY   Right.

GROVE   They either make it explicit or they abandon it altogether.

HALEY   By you proposing they continue it, right.

GROVE   What you're after is for her to pay more attention to him.

HALEY   If they rule out their old pattern, then you say, "If you're going to have a marriage with him not having an affair, then you've got to do more for him. He can be the recreation director, and arrange time together boating, or whatever else you would like." She should either let somebody else entertain him or entertain him herself.

GROVE   One or the other.

HALEY   Yes. It's just how to get that over in some dramatic way.

GROVE (*laughs*) That's a pretty dramatic way.

HALEY Otherwise she'll just get angry if you say, "You ought to do more for your husband."

GROVE Right.

HALEY You first have to have an argument with them that he needs something from a woman that he isn't getting at the moment.

GROVE I say to the wife, "You thought everything was all right at that period."

HALEY "Therefore he was treating you OK from your point of view."

GROVE Which he was.

HALEY "So you either have to change the way you treat him or let somebody else treat him." That is the framework.

GROVE That's me jumping on her.

HALEY Yes.

GROVE God! The hard thing about it is that the couple comes in, and the husband has had three affairs. I wanted to jump on him.

HALEY (*laughs*) That's right!

GROVE But then, that's what she's doing already, so I can't do that.

HALEY That's right.

GROVE God! It's so hard to do that alone, you know that? That is so hard to recognize that when you work alone.

HALEY Well, you can jump on him, but I think all it will do is make him more guilty.

GROVE Right.

HALEY Then he'll reluctantly stay with her, and I suspect that isn't what *she* wants.

GROVE You're right.

HALEY You want them to both voluntarily decide they don't want another person in the marriage. You get them to do that by first proposing to them that they agree to have someone else in the marriage.

GROVE   I understand. But I also think I need to jump on him to do some things. She's mad at him and she can't trust him. I've said to him, "It's going to be on your shoulders to figure out something you can do for her so she can forgive you, so she can trust you again."

HALEY   What would help her to trust him again would be a rule that if he even takes a woman out to dinner, they'll separate, and just split. Affairs are just ruled out.

GROVE   Right.

HALEY   That is, you first push them toward an affair. They reject that. Then you set the rules which apply if they are not allowed to have affairs.

GROVE   She has to do the entertaining, and he has to agree that if she's going to be his entertainer, then he can't go get other entertainment on the side.

HALEY   That's right. Also, when they are out together he has to make it pleasant for her.

GROVE   If she's going to free up her time for him, then he has to make it pleasant.

HALEY   Right.

GROVE   It has to be an enjoyable experience for her.

HALEY   Sure. She should leave the date feeling like that was a very nice experience.

GROVE   Then she'll continue to free up her time for him.

HALEY   Yes. But it might be that they could start some recreation they haven't had before.

GROVE   It's an athletic couple. Right now, she acts like she is just so overwhelmed with everything. I have them agreeing to get a cleaning lady, which will give them more time to spend with each other.

HALEY I think about half the marriages in the country would improve markedly with a cleaning lady.

GROVE Yes. This couple can afford it. They can easily afford it. I'm worried that if they try and split the household work, she'll end up ordering him around and he'll end up not doing it exactly the way she wants, and that will just be a mess. I'm trying to tell them to just get a cleaning lady and avoid the whole thing.

HALEY You know, it also makes him a little higher in the scale if you say that in Europe it's customary for a man to have a mistress and his wife accepts it. It puts him in a mistress class, rather than a man sneaking off to have an affair.

GROVE This is another case where the wife is the more powerful one. I didn't realize that until I saw them together, and he couldn't handle her. That's why you're saying for me to jump on her.

HALEY Or, to not define him as a villain.

GROVE It's yet another case where the husband has to be raised in some way. It's the same old thing about elevating the man.

Follow-Up

I offered several directives to this man and woman which they accepted and turned into something positive. When they first came in, the wife was very angry about the affairs and uncertain about what to do. The husband was feeling very guilty and was desperate to save the marriage. This made for an intolerable day-to-day atmosphere at home. Having them set a time period in which they agreed not to separate but to see if they could improve their relationship gave them some certainty. That took some of the edge off.

The wife was also tormented by thoughts of the affair and was very angry. An intervention was needed to make it clear that the affair was the husband's responsibility and was wrong. I had the couple schedule a specific time each day for the wife to yell at the husband about the affair. During this time, the wife could say anything she wanted, and the husband had to just listen. When the wife's time was up, the husband had to say he was sorry, and nothing else. This helped the wife immensely. Surprisingly, this also helped the husband. Since he felt so guilty, this became like a penance for him. After two weeks of this scheduled venting, the wife no longer felt a need to continue it. To help the wife forgive the husband, and to ensure that in the future this affair would never be brought up again, the husband agreed to take his wife on a summer trip to Europe. The wife was very pleased by this idea.

Although the above tasks were helpful to this couple, the most powerful interventions involved reframing the husband's intentions in a way that elevated the husband. The wife agreed that she was in fact feeling very overwhelmed with work and family responsibilities during the time when the husband was having his affair. This was not, however, a case where the wife did all of the housework and the husband did nothing. In fact, the husband did more at home than the wife. I reframed the husband's having an affair as his way of trying to not put too many demands on her. He was trying to not upset her with any added stress. The wife agreed that this was possible, and this reframe helped the husband move out of the villain class.

Next I talked to the couple about the many ways couples can arrange a marriage. I explained that in Europe it is not uncommon, especially in the upper classes, for the husband to have a mistress, and that the wives are accepting of this. I suggested that in their case the wife was overstressed, so maybe they could just have an agreement that the husband is allowed to have a mistress. I explained that I was not proposing that husbands in general be allowed to have mistresses. If their situation had been reversed, the agreement could be for the wife to have a boyfriend, but since the wife felt the marriage was not so bad while the husband was having an affair the husband's having a mistress might be OK.

As I gave this talk, the wife listened very attentively, with wide eyes. She did not appear to be upset by this idea. The husband, on the other hand, was very upset. At one point he began to cry, looked over at his wife spontaneously, and said, "I don't want a marriage like that." The wife was very moved by this. The couple then decided on the rules they wanted for a marriage with no affairs. The husband did become the entertainment director, and he began taking his wife out on some very romantic dates. The wife made herself available to the husband, and the couple continued to improve. They went on a European vacation together and enjoyed it immensely. After their trip, I continued to work with the couple, focusing on helping them change their pattern of the husband not asserting himself, the wife becoming very upset, and the husband withdrawing. This proved to be the most difficult pattern for the couple to change. Eventually, the husband did manage to find a way to assert himself and the couple ended therapy.

THERAPY AT AN IMPASSE

An extramarital affair is an issue with many couples who seek marital therapy. Therapists seem to agree that trying to help spouses improve their marriage while one of them is having an affair is next to impossible. How to deal with affairs therapeutically, however, is controversial. Often affairs can go on for long periods of time, with the spouse who is having the affair never conceding it to their mate. If a therapist is presented with this situation, one issue is whether the therapist should encourage the couple to discuss the affair openly. Generally, I prefer an approach that stops the affair but leaves the decision about whether to discuss it openly or not up to the couple. This can be accomplished if the therapist meets individually with the spouse having the affair and persuades him or her to recess seeing the other person for the course of the marital therapy. Often, if the affair is recessed and the therapist can help the spouses improve their relationship, the affair is not resumed and the marriage can continue.

An exception to this rule occurs when the spouse who is having the affair agrees to stop the affair but the therapy reaches an impasse nonetheless. This can happen if the spouse who did not have the affair is resentful and unmotivated to initiate anything positive. The therapist is then faced with the dilemma of how to get the unmotivated spouse past the affair issue, when the other spouse has not conceded openly that the affair ever happened. One way of handling this dilemma is for the therapist to meet individually with the unmotivated spouse, let's say the wife, and arrange for her to realize on her own that her husband has had an affair. She can then be sent off individually to think about whether she wishes to continue her marriage or split. This is a very tricky therapeutic procedure.

What follows are excerpts from a case consultation in which Haley outlines how to implement this strategy. The spouses are in their early forties, have been married close to 20 years, and have two children. The wife had been having an affair for several years which she and her husband had never discussed. At the time the couple came to therapy, the wife was leaning heavily toward leaving the marriage. She was willing to stop the affair and come to therapy, but not much else. The husband said he was desperate to save the marriage. I set up a framework where the wife agreed to stop seeing her boyfriend and to give the marriage three months to see if it could be saved. Since the husband said he wanted to save the marriage, I put it on his shoulders to win his wife back. He and I listed several things he could initiate that would improve his marriage. The problem was he did not do any of them. The therapy came to a grinding halt. The husband did not protest to me that the therapy was unfair; he just did not do anything to save his marriage.

GROVE It's been about a month and a half of him doing nothing. I saw him alone and basically beat him over the head individually about how this is the chance he said he wanted to save his marriage and now he's not doing anything. The last time I saw him, they came in together and the wife said she had left him a note one day to stop by and have lunch with her. He didn't do it. He just didn't show up. She then lambasted him in the session, saying, "You want to win me back, but you won't even come over for lunch." I didn't know what to say. I was sitting there thinking, "My God, she's right!" He's depressed and overwhelmed with grief that the marriage might end, but then he doesn't do anything to save it.

HALEY   Are they living in the same house?

GROVE   No, they're separated.

HALEY   That complicates it. He knows about the affair, or doesn't he?

GROVE   He may have figured it out, but it hasn't been made public between him and his wife.

HALEY   The man is behaving like somebody who is very resentful, and I don't think it's just over the wife wanting to end the marriage. He's acting like, "After what you did to me, I'm not going to do anything."

GROVE   That's exactly right.

HALEY   I think you either have to get the affair into it or just go with their splitting.

GROVE   If I wanted to get the affair into it, how would I do that?

HALEY   One way would be for her to list all his faults and end by saying, "That has driven me to be interested in somebody else."

GROVE   My God, that sounds hard.

HALEY   I think if you don't deal with the affair, and that's the issue, the whole strategy isn't going to work. It's not going to do anything.

GROVE   You think the affair is the issue?

HALEY   Something's the issue. Why shouldn't the man stop and see her, call her up, or say, "I'm sorry I was late," you know? He doesn't do the minimum, apparently.

GROVE   No, he doesn't.

HALEY   If he's not doing the minimum, he either doesn't want her back, or he's mad about something.

GROVE   But he doesn't say that. He says he loves her and he wants the marriage to work. He gets all emotional and cries, and spends most of the hour in mourning. But then he doesn't do anything about it.

HALEY   You know, another way to do it would be to leave the wife out of it. I suspect he knows. I think spouses always know if it's an ongoing affair.

GROVE   It would be hard for him not to know what's going on.

HALEY   He knows, he just doesn't want to concede it. You can do an interview where you say there's this mystery. You say, "We've agreed on a plan for what you should do to save your marriage, and you haven't done it. I am worried there is a mystery about something that might be upsetting you." He'll then disagree, or change the topic or whatever, and you always get back to, "But there is still this mystery."

GROVE   No matter what he says, I say, "What about this mystery?"

HALEY   Have him come in alone, and set the interview up for a couple of hours.

GROVE   I just keep saying, "What about this mystery?" until he finally realizes about the affair.

HALEY   That's right. As you keep repeating, "What about this mystery?" he'll have to continue to search his mind.

GROVE   If I spend two hours with him and he realizes that she was having an affair, then what? I remember that Erickson case[2] – he sent the husband away to think. He did an elaborate thing with that couple. I don't remember exactly what it was.

HALEY   He first sent the wife away. Then he had the husband realize she had been cheating on him and had him go home and think over what he wanted to do. That husband decided to forgive his wife and they stayed together.

GROVE   All right. That's what I need to do. If that's what's holding this man back, and he can admit it, then he'll have to do some thinking.

HALEY   If he realizes she had an affair, tell him he shouldn't talk to his wife about this. He should think about it on his own and decide.

GROVE   Why not talk to his wife?

HALEY   He might rush over and have a fight with her. Say to him he first should give some thought to the matter.

GROVE   Yes. Boy, he's going to have to restrain himself for that.

HALEY   If he goes over and makes her mad, and she might say, "We had sex and I preferred this other man to you."

GROVE   She might say that. The couple's sex life has been terrible, even before they were estranged. So I'd be worried that she'd say something like that in a fight.

HALEY   Well, then he has to learn how to deal with her in a different way sexually, too.

GROVE   Oh, I know! But she's not even close to letting him touch her. I'd be ecstatic if I got that far with them. Improving their sex life is the least of my worries right now.

HALEY   I think you should try an interview in which you don't mention anything but this mystery.

GROVE   Suppose he figures this out, and goes and thinks about it. Then if he goes and tells her, one way or the other, whatever his decision is, he's going to eventually tell her, "I've realized this."

HALEY   He may concede he knows it, and decide not to tell her, but try to win her back from the other man anyhow, without ever making an issue of it.

GROVE   What I'm concerned about is that, if he tells her, then she's going to think that I told him.

HALEY   Oh. You can say, "I didn't, he figured it out himself."

GROVE   Yes.

HALEY   You can say you thought about whether to tell him or not. He seemed so reluctant to do anything to improve the marriage that you thought he was angry about the affair, but you decided not to tell him.

GROVE   Yes.

HALEY   But that you did talk to him about, "There's a mystery here," and he came up with it on his own. Which is fair, that happens. On the other hand, if the husband asks you, "Do you think my wife is having an affair with another man?" you'd have to say something like, "Is that possibly what you're thinking? Would that explain why you're so reluctant to do something about it?" That is, you can't confirm it or deny it. That's where you have to keep out of it.

GROVE   Yes.

HALEY   But I think you should do an interview that has one issue. No matter what he says, you get back to, "What has that got to do with this mystery?"

GROVE   Right.

HALEY   No matter what he brings up. You're helping him search the whole situation, and he can then come out from under avoiding it or denying it. You won't help him by saying what it is; he has to say what it is.

Six Weeks Later

GROVE   I had my two-hour "mystery" session with the husband. It was a very interesting session, but he still didn't talk openly about the affair. I gave him two hours. He came so close to it. I told him, "You're acting like a man who doesn't want to stay with his wife. But you say that you do. You're a reasonable man, so there must be some mystery that explains why you're doing what you're doing."

He said, "You gave me a method and I'm not doing it." I said, "Yeah, and that's a mystery, why is that?" He said, "I don't know if I could trust her again." I said, "What do you think she'd do? What don't you trust her about?" He said, "She withdrew from me sexually." I said, "When did that happen?" He said, "Several years ago." I said, "Well, why do you think that happened?" "She had a night job," he said. I said, "Did you accept that reason at the time?" He said, "No." He got so close to conceding it and then he'd change the subject. I'd say, "It's a mystery."

HALEY   Were you listening to him metaphorically or you were listening to him literally?

GROVE   What do you mean?

HALEY   "A night job!" It has its implications, you know.

GROVE   How would you respond to that?

HALEY   I would just say, "A night job?"

GROVE   At the time there was an atmosphere in the room. It was the strangest thing; it was interesting. There was an atmosphere in the room, like there was something, but by God, he wasn't going to say it. He got so close to it. He got right up to it and then wouldn't say it.

He said, "You think there's something I'm avoiding." I said, "If you're avoiding something, it might be something very painful to know." He said, "Do you think I should know it?" I said, "If you really want to know it, if there's something to know that you're avoiding, and you really want to know it, I think you'll figure it out."

It was hard to figure out how to say this to him so it wouldn't seem that I was suggesting what he should do. I decided that there must be a good reason why he's avoiding it, if he's avoiding it this strongly. We went around like this and as he was leaving, he said, "I am acting like I don't want her." I said, "There must be a reason for that," and sent him out. I fully expected that by the next session he would realize it. But the next week he came in and said, "I've thought about this, and I don't think there's a mystery." His attitude had changed though.

HALEY   How so?

GROVE He's decided he wants the marriage to end. When I saw them together again, he even came out and said to her, "You were sneaking around on me." He went that far. But the accusation of her having an affair never was made explicit.

HALEY Well, what did he mean about sneaking around on him? Did he say that in her presence?

GROVE Yes. He said that in her presence. I didn't know if I should push him in her presence. If he had been alone, I would have asked him.

HALEY It's not still going on, the affair.

GROVE No, she agreed to stop it in the first session alone with me. I've seen her alone intermittently since then, and she said, "I did what you said." Originally she was not sure in her mind if she should get a divorce. I made the contract with her to help her get certainty on that. I told her in that first session, "You're always going to be second guessing yourself if you don't give your husband a fair chance." She agreed with that, so I believe she really stopped seeing the other man. They chose three months to be the time that they would work on the marriage. That has ended. The wife is now certain that she wants a divorce. I just had a meeting with the parents and the children this past week, to have them talk to the kids about what's going to happen, and for them to reassure the kids that they'll both continue to be there for them. I had a meeting like that. They were very good together with the children.

HALEY The goal at the moment is to get them to share parenting, but not necessarily to get back together as husband and wife?

GROVE The goal now is to spell out how they are going to share the parenting once they're divorced. But the issue of the affair has never been made explicit. It's still not explicit, but he's mad as hell. She herself says, "He's mad as hell at me."

HALEY You know, thinking of it as a technical problem of how to get a mystery out into the open, the way you described it, it sounded to me like you weren't metaphoric enough. When he says, "a night job," you should just repeat back, "a night job." More complexly, when he said, "Should I know it?" I would have taken that metaphorically, with the two meanings of know: "no" and "know." If he says, "Should I know it?" I think you should respond, "You could 'know' it, or you could say 'yes' to it." That is, I would slip in the other kind of "no." I hadn't realized how important it is to use metaphor when you're bringing out a secret like that.

GROVE   Why did you just decide that metaphor is more important?

HALEY   Just from the way you described it.

GROVE   Because it still leaves something open. If I respond in a literal way, I close a door.

HALEY   It closes it, yes.

GROVE   But if I respond metaphorically, that leaves it open for him to still maybe go through.

HALEY   If he says, "I don't know whether to trust her," and you say, "Trust her about what?" you're pinning him down. But if you say, "It's important to a husband to be able to trust his wife," then it opens up, well, "What would you trust the wife about?" without saying what it's about. I just hadn't realized that. The two of you would share the metaphor without being explicit. Then you go through a metaphor to get him to be explicit.

GROVE   I would wait for him to come up with the explicit thing.

HALEY   If you're pushing him too soon, too literally, he won't say it. That is the way I would think of it.

GROVE   Well, do you think I should still push on this issue?

HALEY   I would, for a little while. If you see him alone, say, "Are you still mad at your wife?"

GROVE   It's so incredible. He described his whole situation, how he buried himself in his work, how she even tried to tell him at one point that she needed him and how he didn't do anything about it. Then she withdrew from him. I said, "That sounds like it was reasonable that she withdrew. But you're acting like it was an unreasonable thing. Why is that?" That's how I pushed him.

HALEY   Sure.

GROVE   He said, "I don't know." He thought hard about it. In this session, there were times where he was off in a trance. There were clearly times when his mind was really working on this.

HALEY   There's another level of this, too. It isn't just that she had an affair. It's that she was disloyal, and that she betrayed him, and that she rejected him. There's all kinds of reasons for him to avoid it, and they all have consequences. If he said something like, "I don't know if I could trust her," you could say, "Some men can trust wives, but they can't forgive wives. Other men can forgive wives, but they can't trust wives." That is, you bring in the consequence if he does face this. If he did admit this, what would he have to do about it? He would either have to forgive her or not forgive her.

GROVE   Now he's making it like the divorce is what he's not going to forgive her for. She's divorcing him, and she didn't give him a chance to fix it. He's not going to forgive her for that.

HALEY   Did she not give him a chance?

GROVE   She gave him these three months. She did give him some chances.

HALEY   You think that the three months was a time for him to win her back. The affair was over for those three months, and he never did anything.

GROVE   Exactly. I told him that in this session, and he recognized it as I was telling him. He said, "You've given me a method and I'm not doing it." He recognized that himself. But in her presence he won't acknowledge that at all. In her presence he acts like, "By God, you just did this, and you didn't give me a chance. I knew I did these wrong things but I think I should be given another chance." That's how he is with her, "You're not giving me another chance, you're just bowing out."

HALEY I'm still thinking of the technical problem. Here's another
way to go when he says, "I'd have to trust her; I don't trust her."
You say, "Did your father trust your mother? Is that part of
your family background?" He then has to think about whether
his father would trust his mother. Then you can get into
whether his father would forgive his mother. I'll bet there was
an affair going on in his parents' marriage. Otherwise he
wouldn't have such a reaction to his wife having an affair.

GROVE The idea is that there's more to what he's avoiding than
just something between him and his wife.

HALEY There's some theme in his life that's very important that
this touches somehow. A theme of betrayal or disloyalty.

GROVE You think I should still push on it?

HALEY If he's still angry, and if that anger might interfere with his
parenting.

GROVE I think it will interfere with his parenting. But they are
doing pretty well as parents. It's so hard to tell.

HALEY Sure. You probably could isolate out his fathering of the
kids from his husbanding and he could do the fathering cheer-
fully. You know, another way you can go about it is, if he's
angry now because she's getting a divorce, you can say, "You
must feel like it's a betrayal that she's really being disloyal to
your marriage by deciding to do this." That is, you throw in
the same words you would use talking about an affair, only it's
about divorce. See if that leads him to say, "By God! She
betrayed me before!"

GROVE What you're saying is that if I open that door again, that I
need to listen to the metaphors that he gives and respond
metaphorically.

HALEY Sure.

GROVE Not go after the literal.

HALEY You respond at a higher level of classification. It's the same
as if a mother says, "This kid is so stubborn, this boy."

GROVE   I say, "Males are stubborn."

HALEY   You say, "Males are stubborn."

GROVE   Well, what will I gain if he realizes about the affair, that's what I'm not clear on.

HALEY   The only thing you would gain at the moment is that, if he realizes it and feels he has to do something about it, he'll have a fight with her about that affair, probably. But then he may forgive her to stay related to the children. It would be a real shame if this continued to eat at him when he was picking up the kids for their visit.

GROVE   It's eating at her. Her fear is that he'll stay angry with her. She knows that he deserves to be angry with her.

HALEY   Sure.

GROVE   At one point she told me that he did ask her during the course of their marriage if she was having an affair, and she told him "No." I was thinking, what if she asked me if she herself should tell him about the affair, and I was thinking about telling her, "If he asks you, you should tell him honestly."

HALEY   If they are divorcing, they should be absolutely honest about it. If they were still going to get together, they might conceal it or forget it and put it behind them. There's another way to do it. If you're talking to him, you might start an anecdote about how couples get into the strangest battles sometimes. Sometimes they lead to divorce, and sometimes they don't. Sometimes they stay together even though they fight about the same thing for years. Then say, "I heard about an unbelievable couple. The wife had an affair with the man's best friend over 30 years ago. Today, they're still arguing about that. Thirty years of arguing! He brings it up at least three times a week, and they have a fight about it."

GROVE   Is this true?

HALEY   It's a true story!

GROVE   Whose case is it?

HALEY Cloé's (Madanes). Thirty years of arguing! She had affairs
with several of his best friends. They're an old couple now,
and they still fight about it. They get violent about it. He hits
her over it. Cloé had the therapist do some romantic things
with the two. When the wife got out of the car, the husband
had to rush over and kiss her as they walked into the restaurant.
She got something going between them. The idea is, if you
can, while ostensibly talking about something else, drop in the
idea about affairs. That's one of the nice things about metaphors and stories.

GROVE So what you're saying is that he may as well face it now,
and just go ahead and be mad at her and holler and scream at
her, if that's what he needs to do. Then, if it's out in the open,
it makes it easier for me to say, "Even though that was a terrible
thing that she did, you still have to talk to her anyway, because
of the kids."

HALEY Sure. If he acknowledges it, then he's got to get past it, if
that's what's separating them. Then they can get past it and
maybe get back together.

Follow-Up

After this consultation, I attempted one more time to get the husband to realize about the affair. He did not, however, admit to me
directly that he knew about the affair. It was my strong impression
that he knew exactly what I was trying to get him to say, but did
not want to bring it up with me personally.

What was important was a major shift in his attitude about the
divorce. He decided that divorce was the best course of action.
Although he was greatly saddened by the end of his marriage, he
was more accepting of splitting up with his wife. I continued to
work with the couple, helping them to construct a co-parenting
arrangement for after their divorce. The children remained in the
custody of the mother.

A follow-up with the man six months later found him to be making several positive adjustments. He was concentrating on his work and had found a new girlfriend whom he was seeing regularly. He and his ex-wife were maintaining the agreements they had made regarding parenting the children, and in fact the man was taking more interest in his children and spending more time with them than he had done during the last several years of his marriage.

5 | ABUSE

NO DESIRE FOR SEX

GROVE I am supervising a case of a married woman who has a
sexual problem and also was possibly sexually abused as a child.
I have live-supervised two sessions with this couple. The family consists of the couple, who have been married for over 15
years, and their two biological children, both boys, ages 14
and 12. It's the first marriage for both spouses. The therapist
began with this family helping them with their out-of-control
14-year-old son. She helped them with their son, and then the
couple asked for help with a sexual problem the wife has had
for many years. The therapist asked for my help with the sex
therapy.

The problem is that the woman has very low sexual desire
and very infrequent orgasms. The husband wants more of a
sexual relationship and she says she has no desire for sex. Until
about five years ago, these two were very serious, longtime
drug addicts. Then, they both managed to kick drugs. The
wife says that the only time in her life when she had any desire
for sex was when she was using drugs. She had no sexual desire
before that, even with previous sexual partners, and has had
no desire since she stopped using drugs.

HALEY Do they have an explanation for that?

GROVE Her explanation is that she thinks something may have happened to her when she was a child. She can't remember her childhood before she was 12 years old. In the session she was obviously entertaining the idea that she had been sexually abused, but she wouldn't come right out and say it. We asked, "What ideas have you entertained about what might have happened?" She would not be specific.

Again, we have these two problems going on at once. One problem is with her current sexual functioning. It looks to me like the couple are in a power struggle around sex. He pressures her for sex and she gives in, but she doesn't enjoy it. Then he's dissatisfied because he really wants to please her. The second problem is she can't remember anything before she was 12 years old. She is relating that to her current sexual problem.

Let me tell you what I set up. I set it up for the husband to help her over the problem of her low sexual desire. The therapist is a woman, so first I had her persuade the wife that she ought to try to overcome this problem. The therapist said, "This is more than a problem that is between you and your husband. This is also about you learning to enjoy and be in control of your own body. It would be a shame if you lived the rest of your life with this problem." While the therapist and wife were talking, it became clear that the wife was afraid that if she became more active sexually she might start remembering painful things from her past. I encouraged the therapist to try to separate her past from her present sexual functioning. The therapist said, "There's no rule that says you have to remember things if you don't want to, and there's also no rule saying that if something did happen to you in your past it has to interfere with your sexual functioning now." The wife agreed with all of that, and agreed to try to solve the problem.

HALEY OK.

GROVE We then met with the husband alone, and got him to agree to help her. We forbid them to have intercourse and instructed them for two nights to get in the nude and take turns touching each other all over, except for the sexual organs. We told them the idea was to teach her how to begin to be sexually aroused.

HALEY   Did they do all of that?

GROVE   They came back in two weeks and reported that the husband had arranged this very romantic evening, which was supposed to end up with this touching exercise. The wife got anxious and did not go through with it. Then, two days later, she felt guilty, and said, "OK, let's try this." They went through the procedure, but at the end the husband wanted to have intercourse. She gave in to having intercourse, and of course did not enjoy it.

Let me tell you the directives I gave, and then I'll tell you what I need help on. We jumped on the husband for having intercourse. We explained that she has to learn to trust men sexually, and that means he may have to sacrifice having intercourse for a while. We then told them to repeat the procedure, but with the wife having total control. She decides what day to do it, and how often.

Now, here's the interesting thing. In the first session, the wife hinted that she may have been sexually abused, but did not come right out and say it, and we did not come out and ask it directly. In the second session she came in and said she suspects she may have been sexually abused by her father. Her father is dead, her mother is alive, and she has a sister. I'm after your comments on what we've done so far, and on how to tie together the current sexual problems with the problem of her having no childhood memories.

HALEY   What's your hypothesis about why she's having the present difficulty with her husband?

GROVE   I think it's a power struggle between them. He pressures her for sex, and she doesn't want to. Then she gives in but hates it. When she's at home during the day, she reads romance novels and gets herself sexually aroused. Then she calls her husband at work and says, "It'd be a good idea for you to come home early today." He knows exactly what that means, and he comes home early. But by the time he gets home, she just happens to be exasperated about the children, and all these other problems, and she's not in the mood anymore. What would you do with this?

HALEY   I would think about how to make sex more sinful. How they could do it in such a way that it's wrong.

GROVE   You mean wrong morally?

HALEY   Something like doing it on the front porch, where they might get caught and there's danger. Or they could do it on the living room rug while worrying about the children.

GROVE   (laughs) Why that?

HALEY   I think it would make sex more exciting, like it probably was for her when she was using drugs and doing the illegal and immoral things.

GROVE   Oh, I see.

HALEY   But also, it would bring out immoral activities that may have occurred earlier. It would help her remember improper sex, if sex was done to her improperly.

GROVE   Do you think I should stick with the touching exercise since we've got them doing that?

HALEY   Yes but I think they need more steps.

GROVE   What other steps?

HALEY   What you're after is for the wife to rebel and say, "By God! We'll do it our own way whenever we feel like it!" The problem is the wife didn't rebel; the husband did.

GROVE   Right.

HALEY   You could have two hypotheses. One is that she's helping him sexually by having low sexual desire. He has a sexual problem and her problem is protective of that. The other hypothesis is that she's feeling that he's taking advantage of her, or it's a power play and he's asserting himself, and she's not going to let him be in charge.

GROVE Right. So the procedure we gave them has given her the control!

HALEY That should help, yes.

GROVE But your twist is for them to do sinful sex. That brings together the excitement she had sexually when she was using drugs and any memories she may have about improper sex in her past.

HALEY While worrying about the kids, they could get undressed, and then run around the house naked and then get back in bed. They can be preoccupied with, "What if the kids wake up and see us running around the house." (laughs) It needs to be something about somebody watching and maybe them getting caught, and being scary, and wrong.

GROVE They both have the hypothesis that she was sexually abused in her past.

HALEY Well, then you have to deal with that. That's their framework.

GROVE I'm trying to separate those two things by saying, "This may be how the problem got started, but it doesn't mean you have to remember your past to get over it now. If you want to remember your past, we'll help you remember it, but that is a separate issue."

HALEY She probably masturbates and has sexual desire when he's not around. For many women, sexual orgasms do not come from intercourse, but from fooling around without intercourse.

GROVE That is what we have them doing with this touching exercise.

HALEY That should help. This brings back a memory of Charles Fulweiler.[1] He had a sample of women who were trying to get pregnant. He gave the couple a special oil and said the husband had to massage his wife's vagina with this oil for 20 minutes to

prepare her for pregnancy. He made it the husband's medical
duty.

GROVE   (*laughs*)

HALEY   All kinds of ways have been tried to help husbands figure
out how to please their wives.

GROVE   Well, here's why I'm raising this case with you. It's another
example where a woman has a sexual problem and also suspects
she may have been abused in her past.

HALEY   That's right.

GROVE   I'm trying to pin you down on what the decisions are that
a therapist is faced with in this situation. One decision is
whether you bring in the woman's family or not. Another is
whether you put your emphasis on the current sexual functioning or on the personal symptoms she might have, like flashbacks, or in this case, no childhood memories.

HALEY   Because of all the literature and publicity about sex abuse,
there are a lot of women who begin to explain their current
problems by past sexual abuse they can't remember. I think in
some cases they haven't ever been abused; they just need some
explanation for what's happening. In other cases they have
been abused and can't remember anything. One thing you
could do with this woman is take her through a hypnotic
procedure to help her remember her past.

GROVE   I'm after your suggestions on involving her family with
this. She is already receptive to talking to her sister about this.

HALEY   Right. That's another way to do it. She can ask her sister,
and if it happened with her sister, it might very well have
happened with her.

GROVE   I'm after some guidelines from you on how to make the
various decisions that you're faced with in these types of cases.

HALEY   I think it's an error for a therapist to assume that a current
sexual problem is caused by past abuse. With a woman who
has been abused, I think it's helpful for the woman to talk

about the past abuse. That often helps her to feel very relieved. But I don't think that necessarily will solve the sexual problem with her husband. A purist family therapist doesn't use a past explanation for a present problem. Family therapy assumes that a present problem is adaptive to a current situation.

GROVE You're also not saying to go ahead and ignore the past abuse.

HALEY Oh no! I'm saying don't make the abuse causal to the current problems in your own thinking. If you want to make it causal in her thinking so she can use that to get over the sexual problem, then that's fine. If she has a theory that if she remembers her past she'll be free and can enjoy sex, then you have to help her remember.

GROVE If she has a need to remember, then we ought to help her remember, right. One problem is that I think she's afraid to remember. We told her, "There's no rule that says you have to remember."

HALEY It's so deep in the culture that past traumas cause present problems that it may be hard to get her out from under the idea that she has to remember.

GROVE You think I'm trying to get out from under too much.

HALEY Possibly. I would say to her, "Let's work both ways on this problem. We'll try to help you remember *and* work on your current sexual problem." Then take her through some procedures that help her remember, including seeing her sister.

GROVE I think there are three problems. One is the current sexual problems she's having with her husband. Two is any personal symptom she is having related to what may have happened to her. In her case, that is her not remembering her childhood. The third problem is how to deal with her family on this issue. The suspected abuser is her father, who is dead. Her mother is alive, and I don't know what her health is. She also has a sister.

HALEY If she was sexually abused, then what is important about her family is that there probably will be some consequences in her relationship with her mother and her sister if she now remembers what happened.

GROVE   The question is whether to involve those two in the therapy or not.

HALEY   I would certainly have her start by talking with her sister only. If she's wrong and she was never sexually abused, and she raises that issue with her mother, she's going to have a very upset mother. The mother would be upset that she would even have the idea that the father would do that. The mother may be remembering the father more and more positively now that he's dead. It may upset her relationship with her mother if she even asks her now if the father sexually abused her. One of the ways to approach her is to say, "There are two problems. One is in relation to your husband. The other is your personal problem with your feelings and your past and your own family. Let's separate those two." You can see her alone for the personal issues and see her with the husband for the sexual issues.

GROVE   The question is to what degree do I involve her mother and her sister in the personal issues about her past?

HALEY   I would get them involved. If she really wants to remember her past and she can't remember, I would bring in the sister, who might remember things that your woman can't, and have them talk about it. You can start by asking generally about their childhood, since this lady can't remember anything. You don't have to start with abuse.

GROVE   You're saying, follow her lead. She's already receptive to talking with her sister, so why not bring in the sister. See what comes out of that, and then decide whether to bring the mother in or not.

HALEY   Another way to think about it is, if you do a sexual procedure with her and her husband and it isn't successful, then you start going larger by involving more people in the therapy—

particularly if she has an explanation about past abuse. You bring in the sister first, and see if it can be resolved with her. If it can't, then bring in the mother and the sister. If you bring in the mother, you could always frame the problem to the mother as her daughter has a problem remembering her childhood and she'd like to just reminisce about it, and try to remember it. The mother could start by helping her remember general things. Was she happy or unhappy in school? Then you could ask the mother what it was like raising her. Did she give her parents any trouble? Was she ever spanked by her father in a way that was really upsetting to her so that she may have put it out of her mind?

GROVE When I frame this to the mother, could I say the daughter's worried something bad may have happened to her?

HALEY Sure. But I wouldn't go right to sex. I would first go to other things that happened.

GROVE Begin with general memories of her childhood.

HALEY Sure. Then at some point ask, "Did anything shocking ever happen to her?"

GROVE I could say she's worried that she's not remembering her past because she thinks something bad may have happened to her. A hypnotic procedure would be to go step by step, where first she remembers something positive, then she can have bad memories, if there are any, and so on. You're saying I should follow those same steps only with the family present.

HALEY Have her remember positive things, and then work your way to more unpleasant things. When the mother trusts the therapist enough to be able to speak to her about confidential things, mother may bring these things up herself. At that point it would be appropriate to have the mother apologize for not protecting her.[2]

GROVE Right.

HALEY In many cases of women bringing this up the abuse has happened, but we've also had some cases in which women felt they were sexually abused, and the more we worked with them, the more gravely we doubted they were ever abused.

GROVE   The difficulty that I've had with these adults coming in with the possibility of past abuse is actually getting the other family members in around that issue.

HALEY   Then you have to decide whether you can help them without the cooperation of the family.

GROVE   What ways have you've used to successfully get those potential abusers in? Have you had many like that?

HALEY   Oh yes. We've had them come in on another basis. We use the same framework as we would in any other case where we invite family members to therapy. We ask them to come in and help with whatever the problem is.

GROVE   That sounds a little bit like an ambush.

HALEY   We had one in which the daughter said she was sexually abused by her father. We brought the parents in, and they just flatly said, "No, this never happened." The daughter said she'd drop the issue if they'd put her through graduate school. The parents had helped her other siblings through school, and the daughter was jealous. She was making an irresponsible accusation toward her parents.

GROVE   What about the cases where you brought the parents in and there really was abuse?

HALEY   With those, usually the client already remembered the abuse when we brought the parents in. It's rare that the client remembers nothing, but suspects he or she was abused, and we bring the family in. Getting back to the marital aspect of this case, I think a woman like this may have a sexual problem with her husband not being desirable to her. She doesn't want to explain it as his not being appealing or attractive. She has to find some other explanation.

GROVE   Or his not knowing how to please her. I think that's more what it is here.

HALEY   That's why you want to change the context of when they have sex, so it isn't the same routine way that is not pleasing to her or that she's bored with.

GROVE   That's why you're suggesting that they have "immoral" sex.

HALEY   Right.

GROVE   We need to help them add some excitement in there. But I think it's also that he just doesn't know how to mechanically bring her to an orgasm. Instead he says, "By God, I want to have sex," and she says, "All right, hurry up and get it over with."

HALEY   "If you have to do it, you won't enjoy it." I worry about these hypotheses about sex abuse because it's in the literature so much. It's a popular explanation for why a couple is having trouble.

GROVE   Or, with this woman, why she doesn't have any memories.

HALEY   One way around that would be to say, "Your past may or may not have been abusive." Then try to get her to agree that she would probably remember a little bit of her past at a time, if she enjoyed sex with her husband a little bit at a time.

GROVE   Tie those two together.

HALEY   Tie them together and help her improve a little bit at a time. I think so much of therapy is one step at a time, incremental bits instead of a massive discovery. You could also do a paradox if you wanted to. Have her avoid enjoying sex, to see what comes in her mind about the past abuse. That would set up her not enjoying sex on purpose.

GROVE   Right. You're hoping that they would say, "This is stupid," and drop their power struggle.

HALEY   Right.

Follow-Up

After this consultation, I supervised one additional session behind the mirror with this couple. The couple had not followed through with the touching exercise, which was intended to arouse the wife's sexual desire and change the couple's patterns related to sex. I decided a new approach was needed to help them with their sexual relationship. Regarding the possibility that the wife had been sexually abused by her father, she continued to have no memory of any actual abuse, but she was more suspicious than ever that she was indeed sexually abused.

Two new directives were given at the end of this session. The therapist discussed with the wife the importance of talking with family members to determine the truth about what may or may not have happened to her. Since the wife herself was unsure, I decided to take a conservative approach and encourage her to start by talking to her sister. The therapist offered to conduct a meeting with the wife and her sister to discuss what the wife's childhood was like and if anything traumatic may have happened to her. The wife agreed to this plan.

A new approach was initiated to help the couple with their sexual relationship. The couple was encouraged to practice "immoral" sex. Examples such as running through the house naked while the kids were in bed or in such a way that they might get caught were suggested. Both the husband and wife laughed at this idea and enjoyed the examples. They spontaneously brought up events from their drug-abusing days, when they had in fact performed "risky" sex. The husband remembered an occasion when they had sex in the bathroom of a restaurant. The session ended with the couple enthused about this idea.

Four months after this session, I called the therapist for a follow-up. Soon after this session, the therapist terminated with the couple, but not before important events had occurred. The wife did talk to her sister, but not in a therapy session. She reported what she had learned to the therapist. She asked her sister directly if her sister knew or even suspected that she might have been sexually abused. Her sister was adamant that she herself had never been sexually abused, and very certain that nothing like that had ever happened to the client. The wife was satisfied with this answer, which apparently gave her peace of mind. She was relieved and, after discussing her talk with the therapist, did not bring up the idea again.

The therapist did not follow up directly on the "risky sex" directive. She did report that the couple seemed more comfortable with each other, had planned a weekend trip without the children, and had rearranged their work schedules so they could spend more time with each other. The therapist felt these changes were very positive signs.

AMNESIA

In 1896, Sigmund Freud presented results of his work with 18 clients, 12 women and six men, whom he stated had all been sexually abused as children by a relative or a family friend.[3] All of the clients came to therapy complaining of obsessional or hysterical symptoms and did not easily recover memories about the abuse. In that paper Freud noted that he had worked with many victims of rape who were seriously traumatized but did not display symptoms similar to his 18 clients. Freud stated that the different reactions of the two groups could be explained by repression. The rape victims who had no serious symptoms could readily recall and discuss the rape. His clients, however, had repressed all memory of the abuse and could only recall it after painstaking hours of analysis. Freud concluded that uncovering repressed memories of past abuse was the central task of therapy with these clients. This idea continues to strongly influence treatment of clients who present a wide range of symptoms, including distress over past abuse. Hypnosis is frequently used to help clients search their pasts as they attempt to discover abuse perpetrated against them in their childhoods.[4]

In Freud's thinking, repression is a term that describes a psychological phenomenon. The term "repression" takes on a different meaning, however, if an interpersonal language is applied. Abuse is "repressed" when it is not talked about among the people knowledgeable of the event. A secret could be described as an interpersonal form of repression. Maintaining a secret is a current behavior in relation to a past event. Abuse victims who suffer greatly as adults can continue to be disturbed by this secrecy. For example, if a woman was abused as a child by a family member, and that abuse remains a secret, her current family relationships can be greatly influenced by the family's denial that the abuse occurred.

In an interpersonal therapy, "lifting repression" becomes breaking the current secrecy and denial of abuse among the group in which it occurred. The main task of the therapy becomes arranging for the family to discuss openly what happened. The victim is validated when the family can acknowledge what happened and place the responsibility on the abuser.

What is the role of hypnosis in this type of therapy? In this approach it is not assumed that lifting psychological repression for past abuse is a central therapeutic task. Some clients, however, come to therapy very disturbed by an inability to remember blocks of their childhood. Our preferred method of helping these clients reconstruct their past is to invite other family members to participate. Then, if abusive episodes are disclosed, the family members are available to acknowledge what happened, place the responsibility on the abuser, and apologize in a therapeutic setting.[5] In some instances, however, it is not possible to bring in a client's family. Family members may be dead, or live in another region of the country, or the client may block an attempt to involve family members in the therapy. Hypnosis can then be offered to help the client remember.

In the following conversation, the client sought therapy for problems she and her husband were having with their daughter. The mother was in her mid-thirties and was grossly overweight. Her daughter was a heavy drug user. When the daughter was hospitalized to detoxify, the mother volunteered to me that she had been sexually abused throughout her childhood by her older brother. She had one older brother and one older sister. Her mother was alive and in poor health. Her father was deceased. She explained that she had never told anyone the story of what happened, not even her husband. Only with great difficulty was she able to tell me what she remembered her brother had done.

Although she could remember the abuse, she was unable to recall much of her childhood and this greatly distressed her. I encouraged her to let me help her put these issues to rest by meeting with her and her family. She was adamantly opposed to this. She was even unwilling to allow a session with just her and her sister.

I consulted Haley, who outlined a simple hypnotic procedure to help with this problem. In Haley's approach, hypnosis is used conservatively, with the goal of meeting the client's individual needs. No assumption is made regarding what the client must remember in order to become a well-adjusted adult. By the end of the therapy with this particular client, no formal hypnosis was used; however, the procedure Haley outlined has been useful to me in helping other clients and in clarifying the role of hypnosis within this approach.

GROVE   This client is 36 years old, and married. She was sexually abused by her brother and was tortured by him for years as a child. She said she's forgotten most of her childhood. She remembers that she was terribly abused sexually by her older brother, and remembers spending hours hiding from him in a closet, but generally she says she has blocked out much of her life before she got married. She got married at age 17 to escape her family. She told me, "I have forgotten much of my childhood and I want to remember." She's wants to go on a mission now to put her childhood in place. The motivation to do that is coming totally from her. I've told her that the best way I know to help her with this would be for her to bring her brother and sister in and for me to help her settle this among all of them. She is absolutely against that. I'm now stuck with trying to help her with this by just working with her individually. I said, "There are probably things that you don't want to remember, and there are probably things that you do want to remember. There's no rule that says what you do and do not have to remember."

HALEY   I'd tell her that as she loses weight, she'll remember.

GROVE   Really.

HALEY   That the weight is a protection against the memories, and
against sex. If she loses weight and becomes more attractive,
she's going to remember more.

GROVE   I'd like to start by giving her some directive that she can
remember without all the affect.

HALEY   I would use hypnosis for this.

GROVE   How would you handle this hypnotically?

HALEY   I would have her remember in stages. Have her relax and
meditate with you first. Give the instruction that you want
her to remember something about her childhood, but you
want it to be only pleasant things first. If there are unpleasant
things, she can remember them later. Say that if she begins to
remember anything unpleasant, she'll start to wake up. Then
you'll relax her again, and she'll just remember pleasant things.
First take her through an hour of pleasant things.

GROVE   Should I specify an age that she should remember, or
should I leave that totally open?

HALEY   See how she does it.

GROVE   She can choose whatever age she wants?

HALEY   Sure. What was the most pleasant memory? She'll pick the
age, or an event like a birthday party. You can give an example,
like her three-year-old birthday party. Have her only do this
with you, and not on her own.

GROVE   Should I have the husband present?

HALEY   I wouldn't, no. This is a private thing.

GROVE   Should I tell her before I have her relax that we're going
to do this in stages and start with pleasant memories only, so
that she knows what to expect?

HALEY   That's right. Then the next stage would be to have her
have some memories, but not have any feeling about them.
She could see them on a screen, like in a movie.

GROVE   She could see herself.

HALEY As a child, yes. But she doesn't have to feel any of the sensations the child felt. She could just be curious about that little girl and what she was going through. If she can see it on a screen, she would be dissociating from it.

GROVE Right. She said one thing she does remember about her childhood was hiding in the closet from her brother. The last stage would be what? Have her remember with affect?

HALEY A little bit at a time, as much as she can tolerate, yes.

GROVE How would you set that up? What would you tell her so that it would be as much as she can tolerate?

HALEY I'd try to do it with every pound of weight she loses.

GROVE That's great!

HALEY I'd tie it absolutely into the weight.

GROVE If she loses three pounds, then how would you say that?

HALEY Well, you could make different degrees of memory. One degree, which would be mildly unpleasant, up to ten degrees, which would be frightening. As she loses one or two pounds, she can have a one or two degree memory.

GROVE That is a really nice way, because I think you're right, that's what that weight is there for.

HALEY You just take it literally. Now it's a metaphor of making herself unattractive so she won't come to any sexual harm.

GROVE Could you just talk more about setting this up hypnotically?

HALEY Well, you mainly tell her to do something deliberately, and then you ask for something involuntary. You ask her to sit in the chair, and put her hands on her knees, and then you say, "I want your eyelids to get heavy. As you meditate, and relax, the rest of you can relax." That is, you go from asking her to do something deliberately to asking for something involuntary, like the heaviness of the eyes or the spontaneous relaxation of her body. Then you say, "While you're relaxing, your unconscious mind can rove over the memories and choose the most interesting and pleasant ones. It will pick one and you'll become aware of it."

GROVE So I could say something like, "As you're relaxing, your unconscious mind can look over the past and pick a pleasant memory."

HALEY You can say, "The back of your mind . . ." so that she would understand it.

GROVE Right, I like that better. "In the back of your mind." I like the terms that are nontechnical. I could have her see the pleasant memories on the screen, too, as preparation for the next stage, when she sees the unpleasant things on the screen. I could have her imagine a movie screen seeing herself having fun times. Should I have her tell me what she's seeing?

HALEY The best thing to say is, "I hope what you remember is something you can share with me." That implies there are other things that she doesn't have to share with you.

GROVE I say, "As you're remembering this, I hope that it will be something that you can share with me." Should I actually ask her to share it with me?

HALEY Well, you need to guide her through it, partly. Because she'll probably say, "I don't remember anything." Then you say, "Well, you remember a bicycle you once had." Or you give her something specific like that.

GROVE I could ask about her first doll.

HALEY Her first doll, her first bicycle, or her favorite doll. As she does that, you can ask her to look around the room and describe where she is. Have her see her bed, and see the wall and the window.

GROVE Suppose I get her to be eight years old with her doll; then what?

HALEY Well, you could either bring her forward or backwards.

It's nice to start back and come forward. It could be the earliest memory of the doll and then later on.

GROVE   If she's eight years old for a while, then I can ask her to go forward to nine, and ask her to have a pleasant memory from that age.

HALEY   Sure.

GROVE   She says that what upsets her most is when she's talking to a girl friend or somebody and they say, "Well, when I was a kid my mother and I used to do such and such." She doesn't have an example that she can use from her past, so she feels odd. She doesn't feel like she's part of the human race because she has this big blank spot.

HALEY   I was kidding my son Andy about amnesia, and I said, "What was the name of your third grade teacher?" He said, "I had two of them, Mr. So-and-so, and Miss So-and-so." He remembers every teacher he ever had. I can't remember my high school teachers' names. So people vary a lot in what they remember. You might have a little discussion with her about memory. Explain to her that some people forget their child-hood, and some remember. Some forget it because it's painful, and some forget it just because they've forgotten. Others can remember every detail.

GROVE   Normalize it for her by saying it varies from person to person.

HALEY   Sure. Tell her if she's forgotten something that was painful, it's for a good reason. She should not just casually remember that. She should only remember painful things if she really wants to and plans to and so on.

GROVE   That's where I get hung up on this. Because I wonder, how much should I push? Should I help her remember some-thing that there's a good reason to forget?

HALEY   Well, you have her remember those things a little bit at a time. You can give the analogy of a jigsaw puzzle. First you get one corner of it done, then you get another corner done. Eventually you discover what the puzzle is.

GROVE   Let me go through this. Stage one is remembering pleasant things. Stage two is remembering some unpleasant things, but not feeling the unpleasantness. Stage three is starting to actually remember everything, the feelings also.

HALEY   If she is ready for them. Many people don't remember everything.

GROVE   I can give her the choice to go as far as she wants.

HALEY   You can say that if you fall down and hurt your knee, the next day you can't remember how that hurt. There's no reason to remember how that hurt. It's something that's past. You can give her a little analogy that it's OK to forget painful things. So if there's some really awful things that he did to her she can forget them if she wants to.

GROVE   I would like to give her the option that she could stop anytime she wants, because I want her to remember only as much as she wants to remember.

HALEY   Right, because you don't know what she wants. There's two aspects of this. One is getting her to remember while she's in a trance. The other is your control of helping her remember after the trance. If she does go into a pretty good trance, she'll remember things. But when you wake her up she'll forget them again. So when you bring her out of it, you have to say, "There are some things that you'll remember today that you'll want to remember and be aware of. Others you may want to forget." That is, you will end up knowing things she won't realize that she remembered when she was in a trance. If you use hypnosis with her more directly, you could bring out all those awful memories and then have her not remember them when she wakes up. With this, since she wants to recover some memories, you have to do it so she can choose the memories she wants to retain from the trance and those she wants to keep on forgetting.

GROVE So when I bring her out of it, I say, "Some of the things that you remember today you'll want to keep on remembering, and others you'll want to forget again." Let her know it's all right to do either one of those.

HALEY One of the reasons for doing that is you don't know what it is about her memories that is painful to her. There might be something you would never think was painful that *she* thought was painful and would like to forget.

GROVE This gets complicated when I think about how to tie all of this to her losing weight. I need a way where it could be tied to the weight or not tied to the weight, either way. Could I say, "As you lose weight, you may remember more, or you may just lose the weight and realize that it's just a bunch of dead weight you've been carrying around after all"?

HALEY Sure. Or those memories are just dead weight.

GROVE She's going to have to deal more and more with whatever it is that she's upset about from her past, or realize that she just isn't upset about it anymore. It's one of those two. That's what I don't want to influence. She may not be that upset about it anymore.

HALEY That's right.

GROVE I don't want to imply that she should be upset if she isn't.

HALEY That's right. You don't want to have a lot of precautions and frighten her. You just say, "People remember when they quiet their minds. So why don't you just relax here for a moment, quiet your mind, let your eyes close, and see what comes to mind. I'd like it to be something pleasant. An early memory perhaps." I think amnesia is the most interesting thing in the business. The way you lift it is by going after details. At least, that's the usual way. You have them remember something, like a doll, and then the room, and then the house. If you just say, "I want you to remember an early memory," she may remember nothing.

GROVE   But when I start giving specific things, and start to ask
about sensations of what she's remembering, she'll start to remember more.

HALEY   Sure. The movie screen is a good idea. You have her see
herself on the screen. Then she's sitting in the audience seeing herself, rather than experiencing it first hand. It's a way of
protecting her, and helping her get an objective understanding
of it.

GROVE   Right. If I start with having her see the pleasant memories
on the screen, then when it's time to remember the unpleasant
things, she has already established that she can watch them on
the screen.

Follow-Up

This client sought therapy primarily for help with her teenage daughter. During the course of the therapy with the daughter, she raised
the issue about her past. I offered several interventions, and she
found some of those interventions useful; however, it should be
emphasized that her primary motivation was to find help for her
daughter.

I offered to help the woman remember more of her childhood and
laid out the step-by-step plan for doing so that Haley had described. I
also gave her several suggestions. I explained that memory works
differently with different people. Some people remember details
about their childhood and others have vague impressions. Some
people forget things from their past because they just forget, and
others forget because their past was painful. I explained that people's
memory of their past varies widely and that it was difficult to say
what was "normal" to remember or to forget. I also explained that it
was OK to forget certain things if she wanted. For example, when
children fall down and skin their knee, if they remember that event
the next day, they do not reexperience the pain. These simple suggestions seemed to strike home for her. She said she would think about

whether she wanted to have a session where she formally would try to remember more of her past.

In a later session she explained that she decided on her own to discuss her childhood with her sister. This was a big decision for her. Her sister helped her remember several positive events from her past. She was very pleased with the talks with her sister. She found it very helpful to discuss her abuse with someone in her family. The client said she had also given great thought to the idea that memory functions differently with various people. She said she no longer felt abnormal that she had such foggy recollections of her past. She seemed satisfied with the recollections she had been able to achieve on her own. After this session, she dropped the issue of wanting to remember more from her past.

TWO STORIES

When an adult comes to therapy presenting the problem of having been sexually abused as a child, he or she can be experiencing a variety of symptoms, such as nightmares, flashbacks, and loss of memory for childhood periods. In addition, dissociative symptoms, such as amnesic periods in a client's current life, are assumed in many therapy approaches to stem from past abuse. The resulting therapy focuses on attempts to uncover past abuse. The client's contemporary relationships are neglected or at best underemphasized. In this book we have emphasized understanding the client's contemporary social relationships as they relate to the client's symptoms and as the target for therapeutic interventions. We view the symptoms related to past abuse as no different from any other symptoms in this regard. With abused clients, as with all clients, we generally assess their contemporary relationships in two areas: their relationships with their family of origin, and their family of procreation, or other intimate relationships.

If the abuser was a family member, and the family is minimizing or denying the abuse, these contemporary behaviors can have a tremendous influence on the client's symptomatology. In addition, it is not uncommon for these clients to report some kind of problem with sexual functioning in their marriage. For example, if a woman comes to therapy reporting current sexual problems and past sexual abuse, she may attribute the sexual problem to her past abuse. A therapist who accepts this explanation and focuses solely on the abuse may overlook sexual problems that the husband is experiencing, such as impotency, inability to maintain an erection, or ignorance about how to satisfy his wife sexually. To avoid embarrassing her husband, the woman will allow her past abuse to be labeled as the problem in the couple's sexual relationship.

One way to approach this problem is to consider the husband a resource for helping the woman over her difficulties. He can be invited to the therapy to help the wife over symptoms she relates to abuse. If the therapist suspects that the husband also has a sexual problem, a sexual procedure can be set up to simultaneously address both the wife's and husband's problems. If the husband does not have a sexual problem, he can still be a resource in helping his wife over her problems and he can be included in the therapy.

What follows are the stories of two women. Both had been very seriously abused sexually by a family member for long periods of their childhoods. Both escaped their abuse when they married as adolescents. Their stories are examples of the consequences of denial by the family that the abuse took place and of the profound role a marriage can have in the victim's success or failure in overcoming the problems related to abuse.

The first woman came to therapy requesting help for her teenage son. She was in her late thirties and had been sexually abused repeatedly as a teenager by her older brother. She never told anyone what her brother had done. She married at age 17 to escape the abuse. Her husband was very soft-spoken and unassuming. The couple developed a marriage in which they avoided each other, including sexually. Her husband never initiated sex and she was very dissatisfied with this. She kept her dissatisfaction to herself, however. She described her husband as "only a friend," saying she did not feel "in love" with him. During her marriage she fantasized about leaving her husband, but felt she should stay with him for the sake of her son. · Throughout her marriage she had regular contact with her mother; this kept alive the legacy of the abuse. Her family's ongoing pretense that no abuse ever occurred continued to torment her and gave an emotional intensity to these relationships which was absent in her marriage.

At the time of the therapy, her son had reached an age where he was preparing to leave home. The woman was then torn between leaving her husband and improving her marriage, which she felt would mean addressing issues related to her past abuse. After I had helped the couple stabilize their son, the woman raised the issues of her past sex abuse and her sexual relationship with her husband. I consulted Haley on the problem.

GROVE She says she can't make love; she can only have sex. She relates that to being sexually abused by her brother.

HALEY I would help her out of that explanation. I would say to her, "Many women feel vulnerable about sex. Some women get scared when they are vulnerable sexually because they don't want to be taken advantage of. Therefore, to get past that you're going to have to go through a period of feeling vulnerable about having sex." Then you can set it up with the husband gradually having more and more contact with her sexually.

GROVE What would you say about the sex abuse?

HALEY I would talk to her about it and have her tell you the story of what happened. You may also have to help her with her family. But after 20 years of marriage, I wouldn't assume the past sexual abuse is causing the sexual problems with her husband. If she has that explanation, then you have to go along with her. But it's not a good explanation for you to have. I would assume the husband has some problem being romantic with her.

GROVE What would you do about that?

HALEY I would set it up by saying that because she was sexually abused, she is anxious about having sex. You could start by saying to them both together that you would like them to make love without having sex. Then, if you wanted, you could put them through stages.

GROVE Do it around him helping her to develop trust.

HALEY Yes, then set it up in stages. Stage one is for them to have four or five nights in which they do nothing but lie down with each other and talk. Next they can make love but not have intercourse. Then, finally they can have intercourse. Tell them you want them to do a little bit every night, or every other night, or whatever they do. It would make sense to her and I think he'd like that.

   She may have been terribly abused and you may have to help her with that, but if you focus only on her past abuse, you end up neglecting her husband. He may have difficulty getting an erection. He may have a real problem of some kind. Her having all this sexual difficulty helps him save face. The couple then never solve the aspect of the problem which is between them.

GROVE Right. When she told me they had sex, I asked her, "How was it?" She said, "It wasn't great, but it was all right." I didn't think to ask about the husband's functioning. You're worried the man may have a performance problem.

HALEY Or, if it's not a performance problem, it's that he gets it up after a lot of effort from her, which she then resents because she feels he should spontaneously come toward her. It just may be that she wants him to initiate sex and he doesn't. She's been waiting quite a while for that and finally she decided to do the initiating.

GROVE Yes.

HALEY Then, no matter how pleasurable it is, it isn't pleasurable because he didn't initiate it.

GROVE She's upset because she had to initiate sex.

HALEY Yes. One way to solve that is to get him to initiate sex by
having him take charge of helping her. I would say to both of
them, "Many women feel vulnerable about sex. A woman
who's been sexually abused feels even more vulnerable." You
bring in the sex abuse as part of your explanation. Then I
would get the man to be more romantic with her. I would see
him alone and suggest that he make love to her *without* sex.
They wouldn't actually have intercourse, but one evening they
just fool around, and play around, but not have intercourse. He
can say to her, "I would like to help you feel more comfortable
sexually, so tonight let's make love without sex."

GROVE I just lay it out so that he has to take the lead.

HALEY Yes. He decides how much each night. Then I would
forbid sexual relations until they've had five nights lying on
the bed. What usually happens if you forbid sexual relations is
the couple then goes ahead and has sex. I would also tell her
that she has to keep repeating having sex until she feels better
about it.

GROVE She'll gradually feel better about sex if she learns to trust
him and starts attaching herself more to him.

HALEY Does she ever see the brother?

GROVE Oh yes. But she sees her mother the most. Her family lives
a pretense that nothing ever happened to her. Her mother be-
rates her and accuses her of not doing anything right. She's
taking all this crap from her mother, while her mother has the
brother up on a pedestal. He's the man who abused her.

HALEY She never told her mother?

GROVE No. She never told anybody. Her father was alive when it
was happening. She was her father's favorite. She said, "If I
had told my father, he'd have killed my brother. So I just didn't
tell anybody." She's lived with this all these years. Getting
married got her out of her family, and ended the actual abuse,
but then there was no purpose for her marriage after that.
Meanwhile, the legacy of the abuse continued to follow her.

The thing that's been more painful to her than the actual sex abuse has been watching the brother become the favorite in the family. No one knows that he did this. Every time she speaks to her mother, her mother brags about something her brother has done. She's had a life of the mother doing this year after year.

HALEY   I think you're going to have to help her with these family issues, in addition to helping her with the sexual problem. In your own thinking, though, I would think of these sexual problems as a separate issue from the sex abuse and family problems.

GROVE   That sexual procedure would have a real powerful meaning for this couple. He knows that she's thinking about leaving him. At one point she accused him of being interested in his secretary at work. She told me she just wanted an excuse to have a fight with him and tell him that she was dissatisfied and wanted to leave.

HALEY   Yes.

GROVE   When they had that fight she threatened to leave him. His response was to write a suicide note and disappear for six hours. He walked around aimlessly. He then came home a total mess. She thought he was out there dead.

HALEY   I think you have to get him to take the initiative in general with her and make him more interesting to her. One of the things I would do would be to put him in charge of the affection each night without sex. You give him a clip board, and have him write down, "Night 1, lie on the bed with the light on, 15 minutes just talking. Night 2, lie on the bed nude. . . ." That becomes his list. Then he checks it each night to see what they're supposed to do that night. That will get a new pattern going of him initiating sex and I think she would like that. I would think of that as a separate issue than the problems related to her abuse.

I presented this sexual procedure to the couple and the wife was very eager to try it. The husband agreed to try to help her. However, after a weak attempt, he again withdrew from his wife sexually. I continued to work with this family primarily around the son. He had been exhibiting very extreme behavior, was in serious trouble with the court, and he was headed toward dropping out of high school. The family worked together and the son stabilized enough to finish school and to avoid trouble with the court. Although the son had improved, he also continued to live at home with his parents. At that point, the family decided to end therapy. The wife decided to remain with her husband, however, and she continued to be very dissatisfied with her marriage.

• • • • •

The story of the second woman has a very different outcome. This woman was horribly abused both sexually and physically by her father throughout most of her childhood. Like the first woman, she also escaped her abuse after she married her husband at age 18. Soon after her marriage, however, she began to experience very extreme symptoms which she related to the past abuse. She took several steps, including going to therapy, to overcome these problems. After over one year of determined work, she was able to overcome her most severe symptoms.

Several years later, she and her husband sought therapy with me after the birth of their first child. The couple were in their mid-twenties and were having serious conflicts with the husband's family. The family was struggling to adjust to the changes associated with the birth of their first child. I worked with the spouses and they were able to make several changes. Therapy was terminated on a positive note. Although the focus of my therapy with them was unrelated to her past abuse, I was impressed with how she had been able to overcome serious symptoms that she associated with the abuse. After the termination of their therapy with me, I invited the wife to meet with me and tell me the story of what happened to her as a child and what she felt was most helpful to her in overcoming her symptoms.

What follows is an interview between myself and the woman which took place several months after the termination of my therapy with the couple. It was held at my request and was not a therapy session.

GROVE I'm interested in your story. We've talked about what life was like for you when you were a girl, growing up in your home. What really impressed me was what happened after you moved out of your parents' home. Could you tell about the problems you were faced with after that and how you were able to overcome them?

KAREN You would like to know what I went through after leaving the home, after my husband and I got married?

GROVE What were the problems that you were faced with then?

KAREN In my marriage, the abuse from my father affected our being intimate with one another. I also had a hard time with trust. I always wanted to do everything at home. I worried if I failed in any way my husband would leave me.

GROVE If you weren't perfect he would leave you.

KAREN Exactly. I constantly strived to be this perfect person. I was the same way with my in-laws—with just about all of my relationships.

GROVE How do you relate the idea that you had to be perfect to what happened to you?

KAREN Growing up, I never knew when dad was going to blow up, or what nights he was going to be waiting for me in my room. I thought that if I did everything perfectly during the day, I might escape being abused at night. Sometimes he would come after me anyway. But usually if I would do everything perfectly that day, I would get out of being either physically or sexually abused that evening. One of the things that my father was notorious for was game-playing. I would walk into my room, I would think that he wasn't there, and he would be hiding someplace. That was his game. He liked to be the hunter. That was my total experience with men, so the first two years of my marriage I thought I had to be perfect. An extreme example was that I would mop my floors every day. I would clean, vacuum, and dust every day.

GROVE After you were married?

KAREN Right! So he'd come home to a perfect house and a perfect wife. But then he would want to be intimate and I wouldn't be able to function. I would function, but I wasn't functioning. I completely shut down during our sexual times together.

GROVE I want to ask about that if it's all right with you. But I also would like to find out what happened that finally convinced you that you could trust your husband and that you didn't have to live with the worry that he might leave you if you weren't perfect.

KAREN After my husband and I had been married for about a year I got therapy. I went to therapy on the pretense that I was a habitual liar. I believed the things I had said about my father were lies.

GROVE You didn't believe those things ever happened.

KAREN No! I couldn't believe anything that horrible could happen.

GROVE Once you got away from your family you started to doubt your own experience.

KAREN Very much so. My family totally denied that anything ever happened to me.

GROVE Did your husband believe you?

KAREN Yes he did.

GROVE But you were faced with this continuous rebuttal from your parents.

KAREN Right. On the outside my family looked wonderful. Everyone around me was saying, "Your family's nice." Everyone saw us as a perfect family. My dad was this outgoing, highly respected, prominent man in the community, but I had this awful image of him.

GROVE   None of your siblings validated that the abuse happened?

KAREN   No, not at all.

GROVE   So you went to a therapist saying, "I must be crazy, I don't know if this happened or not."

KAREN   Right. "I have a very big problem, all I do is lie." I was also having insomnia. I was up most nights.

GROVE   You were having all kinds of symptoms?

KAREN   I was also having eating disorders. I would binge and then purge. Sometimes I would binge and use laxatives. Sometimes I would starve for two and three days. My parents starved me a lot.

GROVE   Did you ever have any nightmares or flashbacks?

KAREN   That was the insomnia. I didn't want to go to sleep so I wouldn't have to have the nightmares.

GROVE   You said you were also dysfunctional sexually.

KAREN   I was very dysfunctional. We had a sex life, but during the first years of my marriage I don't remember half of it. Mentally I just left most of the time. I went to my safe place.

GROVE   What was your safe place?

KAREN   In "Little House on the Prairie," the little girl runs down a hill with this big field of flowers, that was my safe place.

GROVE   You mean during sex you just imagined yourself being there?

KAREN   Right. I just completely blocked out the experience.

GROVE   Did your husband know you were doing that?

KAREN   No. He didn't even know until last year that I cried after our sexual experiences.

GROVE   Did you ever initiate sex?

KAREN   Never.

GROVE   Your husband always initiated sex and you felt you had to comply?

KAREN   Yes. I played the part very well.

GROVE   At this point in your life, can you enjoy sex?

KAREN   Yes, very much so. I can enjoy sex and I can initiate it. I can even feel very comfortable being the more assertive partner. There are still days that I feel like I did five years ago. Because you can never forget what you went through. There are always days when I feel a little insecure.

GROVE   Your family is continuing to deny this?

KAREN   Very much so.

GROVE   At this point in your life you are in a situation where they have not fessed up and taken responsibility for what has happened. Given that, it doesn't surprise me that you still have some insecure days.

KAREN   Right.

GROVE   Do you still have the insomnia?

KAREN   I have nightmares from time to time, especially if I get a phone call from my family.

GROVE   But you don't have the fear of going to sleep?

KAREN   No, and I don't have a fear of my father. When I see him, I don't become this seven-year-old girl who is incapable of taking care of herself, or saying "no," because I know I'm an adult.

GROVE   You're not that little girl anymore.

KAREN   Right. What did that for me was confronting my father, looking him in his eyes, and saying, "You raped me—for years."

GROVE   That was a big step. What other things helped out?

KAREN   I became more secure about myself. I was able to look in the mirror and say, "I'm not a bad looking person; if my husband left me I would be able to find another relationship."

I was never able to say that before. I'd look in the mirror and I would not see who everyone else saw. I would see this really ugly, insecure, stupid person. I'm a fairly intelligent person.

GROVE   What do you think happened that you were able to develop a stronger self-esteem and self-confidence?

KAREN   That came over a long period of time. I put a lot of work into that.

GROVE   How has your husband supported you on that?

KAREN   He was very patient, especially during the year of my therapy. There were days I just could not function. The memories I had and the overwhelming grief were too much.

GROVE   When you went to therapy you started remembering more?

KAREN   Yes. I began to remember a lot more. I remembered that I had gotten pregnant by my father. I had forgotten about that. I never carried the baby to term. I had a miscarriage and I remember my mother and father just being crazy. In fact, they never took me to a doctor. I had developed a very serious infection and a few months later that landed me in the hospital for close to two weeks.

GROVE   You had forgotten about that completely?

KAREN   Completely. I remembered being in the hospital. The doctors couldn't pinpoint what was wrong with me. My parents would never leave the hospital room to allow anyone to really examine me.

GROVE   Why do you think you remembered that?

KAREN   I think I needed to.

GROVE   Why?

KAREN   To get on with my life, I had to know what happened to me, face it and to go on. When I first started therapy, I never thought I'd be able to say, "This is a part of me. This is a part of my past. I've dealt with it and I can go on. It wasn't my fault. I couldn't help what happened." I can only be responsible for what I do with it now. That could either be destructive or helpful. That's how I look at it. I can use my experience and help other people. It's awful what happened. It never should have happened. No person should ever have to go through it, but I did.

GROVE How do you explain having those memories return after you began therapy?

KAREN In my family I was really the only one who would ever fight back with mom and dad. I think that whether I was in therapy or not, I would have remembered. I'm just that kind of person. One day, for instance, my dad had broken my nose, I think it was the second time.

GROVE He broke your nose two times!

KAREN Actually three. I remember that day, even after he did that, he started in on my sister and I said, "Can't you ever stop?" I would stand up to him in public where none of my siblings would. I was the only one who would turn him to children's services.

GROVE You think that because of the type of person you are, after you left home, you had to face what happened.

KAREN Right. That's the kind of person I am. I needed to know what happened. I wanted someone to validate what I was remembering. What I remembered was so horrible. I couldn't imagine those things ever happening to anyone. I couldn't imagine parents not feeding their children. I couldn't imagine parents physically abusing them. I can remember days where I was abused for such a long period of time, I would get to a point where I would just completely lose my mind. Your body and your mind can only take so much before you become oblivious to what goes on.

GROVE After that background, what do you think helped to change your ability to have an intimate relationship?

KAREN At first, after I was married, I was afraid to go out and socialize with other people. I felt so different. Then, when I

started getting out, I found that I was no different from anybody else. We're all just trying to survive. After I began to
work, I would get a wink from someone, or someone who
didn't know I was married would ask me out. I realized, "Gee,
I must look OK. I'm impressing somebody." Or, if I would get
a raise I realized, "Wow, I am OK at this." I would bring that
home with me. The security would build. But, even with all
of that, I was still so angry with my parents.

GROVE   You think that's the reason why you had to go to your
safe place during sex?

KAREN   Oh yes. I was so angry. First of all my dad raped me, and
the same act, really, was what my husband was doing. Not in
the same way, but it was the same sexual act.

GROVE   If you would really be there during sex, you would remember all the things your father had done?

KAREN   It would be too much, yes. I don't think I could have
been sexual with my husband and not remember. Sometimes I
would see my father's face on my husband's body. That's when
I would go to my safe place.

GROVE   You would actually hallucinate seeing your father while
having sex with your husband?

KAREN   Yes. The way my dad's skin smelled would come back.

GROVE   The sensations of sex would bring back all of those memories. That's what you were escaping from.

KAREN   Yes. During sex, at times I could say to my husband, "I'm
not able to handle that. That reminds me of something."

GROVE   Then he would accommodate you?

KAREN   He would accommodate. Telling my husband the story of
what happened helped a lot, too.

GROVE   Your husband helped you by cooperating with you sexually and respecting what you could not handle. Also, it helped
you to just tell him the story of what happened to you.

KAREN   Yes. Some of it is so private and so personal, and so awful.

But I'm a very open person. When somebody asks me, I will say, "I'm a sexual abuse survivor and these are the things that happened." I don't feel ashamed about it now.

GROVE It isn't some terrible shameful thing that you feel wrong about. Your father was the one who was wrong.

KAREN Right. You think no one can love you for those horrible things that you had to do to survive. I did bargain with my dad. I did say, "If you'll leave my little sister alone, you can do this to me as much as you want."

GROVE Then you felt that was your responsibility. When that's just crazy! He shouldn't be doing anything like that to begin with!

KAREN Exactly! But I would bargain with him so he would leave my little sister alone. Then in turn I felt as if I was asking for the sexual abuse.

GROVE Once you got away from your family you started to realize that when you're an adult you have to be responsible. Then you related that to your dad.

KAREN A lot of people look at me and say, "How could you not know that was not normal?" My father sexually abused me until the day I left home. I was 17 at the time. I told my grandfather. He was a minister. He said it was God's punishment towards me.

GROVE It was your total experience.

KAREN Exactly. That was my life experience.

GROVE But when you got away from that and had other relationships you started realizing otherwise. You realized, "This wasn't my fault." But, you had a period of a year and a half where you were struggling with this.

KAREN After I was married, to protect my sister who was still at home, I organized a hearing in court. I struggled clear up until the time of that hearing. I had improved some before the hearing, but I still struggled. But at the hearing, I got validation from my dad. I was able to stand up to him and say, "I'm an adult and I can take care of myself. You can't hurt me anymore."

GROVE   That hearing was a climax.

KAREN   Definitely. It sent a message to my family. It said, "You have been inappropriate. You were wrong." The hearing said to them, "I'm not fucking around with this anymore!"

GROVE   You were willing to say that in public. I think that was a very courageous thing, but it was also a very powerful thing.

KAREN   It gave me a lot of power. They don't screw around with me as much anymore.

GROVE   You stood up to them in front of a lot of other people.

KAREN   All their peers. They knew the judge. They knew the children's services workers. I said, "This is what happened to me. I know this is continuing to happen at home. Whether you want to deny it or not, I know what is going on." As a kid growing up at home, I would report them to children's services. Children's services always said to me, "We can't do anything because we don't have enough evidence." Then, before the hearing, the judge brought me back into his chambers and said, "I don't think I can do anything." I said, "If you don't do anything, I'm going to hurt your election." All of a sudden I had this power. I told him, "Yes, you can do something. This is your responsibility." They didn't want a hearing in the first place.

GROVE   How did the judge change that?

KAREN   All of a sudden I had all of these helpers.

GROVE   What do you mean, all of these helpers?

KAREN   The prosecuting attorney and the assistant prosecuting attorney. I reported that my parents were abusing my sister and they said they didn't have enough evidence. I did it to protect my sister. I went with children's services while they interviewed my sister. My sister wouldn't say that dad had raped her,

although she did say it to me. She just said that dad had forced
her to put her head in his lap. They didn't want to press charges
and bring him to trial.

GROVE At what point in that process did you talk to the judge?

KAREN After I talked to children's services he invited me to talk
with him in his chambers. He said, "I don't know if we can do
anything." I said, "If you don't do anything there's going to be
problems with your election."

GROVE That was incredible!

KAREN The League Against Child Abuse helped me with that. I
also acquired an attorney. So many people don't want to talk
about incest or rape or child abuse. A lot of people can't deal
with it at all. Instead of being supportive, a lot of people just
withdraw.

GROVE They don't know what to say.

KAREN They really don't. It's not a disease. It's not something that's
going to rub off on you. It's just something that happened to
me.

GROVE It was the pretending that it didn't happen that was very
painful.

KAREN Yes. I think what's sad is that most of my sisters who live
outside the home are so upset. My oldest sister is so angry all
of the time. Her life is consumed with anger. She's angry with
everything and everyone. Unfortunately, as much as I'd like to
see it, I don't think my father is ever going to pay for what
he's done in my lifetime. Or in his lifetime.

GROVE What happened that day in court may be the most you're
going get. He didn't admit that he did it. He didn't say, "It was
my responsibility." He didn't apologize. A lot of things didn't
happen. But what you're saying did happen was: You were
able to confront him publicly and how he reacted was enough
for you. It showed you that you weren't crazy. He was the
one who was crazy.

KAREN   Definitely. I still get angry, though, because I don't have a family I can go to like on those holiday TV commercials. I can't have that kind of family. I get angry when I feel insecure about my mothering of my daughter. I never had role models of my own. I feel grief a lot of times for things that should have been and for things that aren't ever going to come.

GROVE   Well, you never know what's going to happen. When your sister is out of the home, that's going to be a new situation for your family to face. Right now you've got the worry of your sister being there. Once she's out of there and free of that you may have another chance. I think if you had just one other sibling who would respond the way you have, that might get all of the siblings to rally around you. That may change how your parents are handling this.

KAREN   Maybe.

GROVE   I think it's incredible that you were able to make the changes that you've made. I've met a lot of women who have experienced terrible abuse and weren't able to have much of a sexual relationship with their husbands.

KAREN   I didn't want to give up any more of my life. My parents took so many years from me, I didn't want to give up any more. Sometimes I still question whether or not I'm accurate in my memory of what happened.

GROVE   Even now, you're not sure yourself?

KAREN   I have days when I say, "Am I accurate in this?" But I think what I have to rely on is my gut instinct.

GROVE   You might not be exactly sure about what it was, but you are sure that something terrible did happen.

KAREN   Right.

GROVE   When you're reflecting on this, trying to identify the changes and the actions that you took that helped you over the symptoms you were suffering from, the court day was big.

KAREN   Yes.

GROVE Another big thing was remembering what happened and telling your husband.

KAREN Exactly. And talking to other people and knowing what their experiences were. Being open and saying, "I experienced this. I'm not really ashamed of it, but it is something that did happen."

GROVE Even now, you still have some uncertainty about exactly what happened. What helped you start to realize that the abuse really did happen?

KAREN I'd been in therapy for about six months. It was my birthday and my husband and I drove to my parents' home. It was snowing that day. I went upstairs to my old room and I became so overwhelmed. For some reason something just said, "It did happen. This happened." All of the screams, all of the cries, all of the terror that I felt when I was in that room all came back.

GROVE That's where it all happened?

KAREN Most of it. My dad also locked me in the cellar a lot. I walked downstairs to the cellar and I saw the broken glass around the door handle, because one day I'd broken the glass.

GROVE That glass was still there?

KAREN It was still broken.

GROVE You saw actual evidence of acts that you were remembering.

KAREN Right. It was a rare occasion for us to go back to their house. After I went down to the cellar I walked out of the house and I stood in the middle of the yard. I started screaming, "It couldn't have happened. I don't want it to be true." Then I started sobbing. I said, "It's true. It happened. This is what happened to me." That's when my grief started. That's when the anger started; more than anger, it was fury. I was furious for years.

GROVE Would it be fair to say that that court date was a day where you could get rid of that fury?

KAREN   That was the climax.

GROVE   You took an action that relieved you of that anger.

KAREN   Right. It was also the time that I said to my family, "I am not afraid of going public with this. I am not afraid to let people know what you are about."

GROVE   When did you stop having to go to your safe place when you and your husband were having sex?

KAREN   I stopped going to my safe place during the time my husband and I were on vacation in New England. We had a whole weekend together. Because of my work, we hadn't seen each other in a month. That was the first time that I don't remember dissociating all or most of the time during sex. I was with him totally.

GROVE   What was it about that time?

KAREN   For the first time in my life I was many states away from my family. I didn't have to worry about the phone ringing beside me, wondering who it was. People respected me and I felt very secure in myself.

GROVE   You had a base of friends. You had a major change of surroundings.

KAREN   Right. By then I also recognized that on certain dates I'm not going to be able to be intimate. I could communicate that with my husband and he would say, "OK, we'll do it another weekend." I think, if women or men can say that to their partners and their partner can respect it, that helps a lot.

GROVE   You were fortunate that your husband did not withdraw from you sexually.

KAREN   My husband did go through a time when he was scared to have sexual contact.

GROVE   Were there times when you wanted your husband to initiate sexual relations and he didn't?

KAREN   Oh yes. During the time when I was remembering all the abuse, he didn't want to make me feel uncomfortable, or hurt me. He didn't initiate sex for a long time and I got real frustrated. I thought, "He doesn't want me anymore. Maybe I've put on too much weight." So we sat down and we talked about it and he said, "I'm afraid. I don't want to hurt you." I said, "But you have to trust that I'm going to be able to tell you if I can't handle sex. That's my responsibility."

GROVE When you were in New England and were able to have your first sexual experience with your husband where you did not have to escape to your safe place, when did that happen in relation to these other events?

KAREN That happened after the court hearing.

GROVE After the court hearing? Let me make sure I understand this. Even after you had a flood of new memories, and after your day when you went to your house and recognized something terrible did happen, even after all of that, you still were unable to have a sexual relationship with your husband where you could really be there.

KAREN Right. We went through stages. At the beginning of our marriage, I constantly dissociated and went to my safe place. I was constantly there. Then we got to a point where I would be there some of the time, but not all the time, but I would always still cry after all my sexual experiences. It was very rare when I didn't. Then we had the court hearing. My husband was in the courtroom. We were able to look at one another. He was able to give me strength. Then I was able to say, "I can trust him. He didn't walk out of the courtroom that day."

GROVE You weren't sure if he would be able to handle that?

KAREN No. Especially some of the questions that my dad asked.

GROVE What questions did your father ask you?

KAREN He said, "Are you saying that I raped you?" I said, "I'm saying that you raped me. I'm saying that you physically abused me." He said, "Well, if I raped you then you must know how big my penis is." The judge was so overwhelmed by that. Everybody was so shocked. I just sat there. I looked at the judge. He wasn't saying anything. I said, "Do I have to answer that?" The judge said, "No! That's inappropriate." Then my father said, "What did it feel like for you then?" I said, "I'm not going to answer that one either."

GROVE He didn't deny that he abused you?

KAREN He did deny it, but in a sense he admitted it. If a father was "normal," he would never ask his daughter those questions. A normal father would never ask his daughter, "What kind of sexual things did we do together?" No father would do that.

GROVE They would just say, "This is crazy, it didn't happen."

KAREN Exactly.

GROVE That court date changed your relationship with your family and also strengthened your relationship with your husband.

KAREN Right.

GROVE I have to tell you, I think you are fortunate to have your husband. You could have ended up with a husband who would not have been patient with you sexually, or a husband who would have withdrawn from you all together.

KAREN I would say to those women who have that experience, because I have friends who are in relationships like that, that you have to decide if that's the kind of relationship you want to stay in. The unfortunate part is, if he's not going to be capable of having a sexual relationship, you're always going to be stuck in a mode of not being able to make love.

GROVE The way you're describing this is that one of the things that allowed you to get through this was your relationship with your husband. Your marriage was a vehicle that allowed you to test out a lot of things and do a lot of different things that helped you get through this.

KAREN Definitely.

GROVE Had you not had that, do you think your efforts would have been handicapped?

KAREN Definitely. If I hadn't had someone who respected me when

I said, "This is not OK for me," that would have broken down our relationship.

GROVE I see.

KAREN Now we recognize that marriage is a day-to-day process. You always have to work on it, 24 hours a day. You have to talk so much with your partner to find out where they're at.

GROVE You can't assume.

KAREN You can't ever assume. Sometimes it's a real bummer because I know for me as a woman, I want that romantic thing, saying, "Oh please read my mind, and know what I want, and romance me." Sometimes he'll do it, but chances are it's not going to happen. (*laughs*)

GROVE (*laughs*) Sometimes men don't pick up on those signals!

KAREN Exactly. It helps when I recognize that and realize it's just a part of the relationship, those are just relationships in general. When my husband and I think that our marriage is at its worst, I remind myself that I do have a relationship that's very different and unique from anyone else's.

GROVE The two of you have a very powerful relationship.

KAREN We do.

GROVE I couldn't imagine otherwise because of what you two went through together. One positive legacy of your past is that it allowed you to attain a relationship with your husband that a lot of couples never attain. They don't ever have to go through that kind of a shared experience.

KAREN Right. Our relationship can be very intimidating to other people. Because we have gone places where other couples have not. You know, we renewed our vows in the church.

GROVE When did you do that?

KAREN Three years ago. We renewed our vows in the church, because I never had a wedding. I wanted to have a wedding because I felt like that was one thing my parents had taken from me. So we did that.

GROVE That's great! I really appreciate you coming down here and
     telling me your story. I learned a lot from you today.
KAREN I'm glad. I've enjoyed doing it.

For both of these women, the abuse they suffered was long-
standing and severe. They both escaped their abuse by marrying at
an early age. Both of their families continued to deny the reality of
the abuse. This ongoing denial had a profound impact on both
women. The first experienced great resentment and anger with every
contact she had with her mother. This kept her focused on the past
and sapped energy she could have devoted to her marriage. She was
unable to confront her family's denial and this resulted in her pain
continuing.
     For the second woman the family's denial had even more extreme
consequences. She left home suffering from a variety of severe symptoms, including doubting her own mind. Although her remembering
the past abuse was a profound experience for her, it did not result in
her overcoming her sexual problems or her gaining confidence in
her memory of the past. These changes only occurred after she
confronted her father in a public setting. Her courage in taking this
step allowed her to move on in her life, and her father's response to
her confrontation gave her some validation that her memories were
correct. This confrontation was an intervention in her contemporary
relationship with her father, not an exploration of the past.
     A major factor in the success or failure of both women in over-
coming their symptoms was the sexual response of their husbands.
Both husbands believed their wives' stories and offered support. Their
sexual responses, however, were very different. The first husband
withdrew from his wife sexually. Despite my efforts to change this
and the wife's desire for this to change, the husband continued to
withdraw sexually. His continued withdrawal increased my suspicion
that he himself was having some type of sexual difficulty. The second
husband was very patient and cooperative with his wife sexually.
Although he withdrew briefly, he responded to her request to continue initiating sexual relations. The couple's sexual relationship pro-

vided the woman with a source of motivation to overcome her symptoms and a vehicle to guide her actions.

CAN ONE PERSONALITY BE ENOUGH?[6]

A 35-year-old single woman brought her 13-year-old son in for therapy. The son was behaving like a juvenile delinquent, and the mother was letting him get away with murder. The boy's father disappeared shortly after his conception, never to be heard from again. The mother's parents were both dead. Her father died when she was a child. Her mother died ten years prior to the time of the therapy. Besides this mother and her son, the only other family member in the area was the mother's younger sister. The mother also had a brother who lived in another state.

The therapist worked with the mother, won her trust, and helped her to settle her son down. At that point, the woman, Betty, began to complain of some very bizarre occurrences. She found matchbooks with men's names and phone numbers in her purse. She did not know who the men were or how the matchbooks got in her purse. In the mornings, she began to find her car parked in a space where she did not leave it the night before. One morning she awoke lying crossways on her bed, dressed in clothes she never wore and did not remember putting on. She discovered bruises on her neck and breasts which she could not explain. It appeared as though she had had a sexual encounter which she could not remember having and this frightened her. The most frightening episode occurred when she "came to" in a bar sitting next to a man. The man told her she had been talking to him for 45 minutes. She did not remember the conversation, how she got in the bar, or what she had done prior to going to the bar. Before "coming to" in the bar, the last thing Betty remembered doing that night was getting in her pajamas and going to bed.

Terrified by what was happening to her and realizing that everything was happening at night, she first thought she was sleep walking.

She put bells on all of the doors of her home, thinking that if she tried to "sleepwalk" out of the house, the bells would awaken her. Also, every night she gave all of her money and her car keys to her neighbor, with instructions to not give them back to her until morning, no matter what.

The therapist asked Betty what her explanation was for these episodes, and Betty explained that when she was 13 years old, she invented an imaginary persona named "Candy." As a teenager, starting when she was about 12, Betty had been very seriously abused by her mother. The mother not only physically abused Betty but also prostituted her to local men in order to get money to support an alcohol addiction. Betty explained that she invented "Candy" to protect her from this abuse. She would go out socially and call herself "Candy." As Candy, she was outgoing and gregarious. As Betty, she was shy and unassuming. As Candy she was involved with boys and experimented sexually. As Betty she was withdrawn socially. Betty explained that when she became 18, she got away from her mother and no longer felt she needed to become Candy. Between the ages of 18 and 35, Betty assumed Candy was gone. Now, however, with these bizarre episodes, she feared Candy was back, taking over her body outside of her awareness and her control.

The therapist was skeptical of this explanation and suggested to Betty that she might be experiencing black-outs from heavy drinking. Betty explained that she did not drink. The idea that she was having black-outs gave her no peace of mind, and after this session she continued to keep the bells on her doors. To convince the therapist about Candy, Betty brought in letters which Candy had written to boys as a teenager. The handwriting was not Betty's. At this point the therapist was convinced that Betty was experiencing dissociated states and asked me to supervise the case from behind the one way mirror.

I consulted Haley about this woman (the first two consultations on this case were not taped) and gave the above description of the problem. Haley insisted that the client possessed multiple personalities and suggested that the first step would be to contact and talk with Candy. I had never worked with a multiple personality client before and was searching for a general approach to the problem. In my first consultation about this case with Haley, he described an approach to the problem which he had learned from Milton Erickson. Erickson had worked with approximately 22 multiple personality clients. Haley explained that Erickson did not approach the phenomenon of having more than one personality as a form of psychopathology. Instead, Erickson would treat the problem as the client actually possessing two or more personalities which happened to occupy the same body. Haley explained that, in Erickson's approach, the goal was not to try to merge the personalities or to search for additional personalities. The goal was to persuade the personalities to communicate directly with each other and to learn to collaborate while sharing the same body. Haley suggested that in this case we would first have to make contact with Candy and gain her trust and cooperation. Since as a teenager Candy liked to write letters, Haley suggested that we try to communicate with her through automatic writing. He then outlined a hypnotic procedure for allowing Candy to communicate through automatic writing.

After several intense conversations with the therapist, I persuaded her that to help Betty we would have to talk to Candy. The therapist was skilled at relaxation exercises, and Haley's automatic writing procedure was adapted to what the therapist was able to perform. The therapist then persuaded Betty to allow her to attempt to communicate with Candy, and a special session was set up with the goal of communicating with Candy. I supervised from behind the mirror.

Betty trusted the therapist immensely; otherwise this whole procedure would not have been possible. Betty was very concerned about whether she would be aware of what Candy said if Candy did communicate with the therapist. Betty was told that she would know what she could tolerate knowing and would not know what she was uncomfortable knowing. This gave Betty the reassurance she needed to proceed. She was then relaxed and sent to an uncle's orchard, which she described as her favorite place as a child. While Betty was relaxing in her orchard, Candy was given a pencil and paper and asked several questions. Candy responded to all of the therapist's questions without hesitation, writing in her own unique style. After a few minutes of this, the therapist thanked Candy for coming and asked for Betty to come back to the room.

When she awoke, the client glanced around the room with a puzzled look on her face. She discovered she had glasses on and abruptly removed them, threw them on the floor, and announced in a thick southern accent, "I hate these dang things!" When asked who she was, the client responded, "I am Candy." Both the therapist and I were startled by this unplanned visit, but after we regained our composure we managed to establish a positive relationship with Candy and got an agreement from her to return to talk with us in the future. Candy had a totally different manner from Betty. She had a different body posture, spoke in a different accent, and presented herself as much more assertive. Before leaving, Candy confirmed that she was indeed going out at night and picking up men. She complained about the man who left a "hicky" mark on her neck, because she knew Betty would discover it. She complained that Betty never allowed her to be in control of the body anymore, so now she had to take over when Betty was asleep. She also said emphatically that Betty had not told us everything, but would not elaborate on what Betty was withholding.

After a few minutes, Candy explained, "Betty's heart's pounding. She's scared and she wants to come back." The therapist then brought Betty back into the room. Betty had total amnesia for what had just occurred. The therapist explained that Candy had indeed communicated and had written answers to questions on a piece of paper. Betty did not want to see what was on the page. The therapist explained that it would be necessary to talk with Candy again in the next session, and Betty reluctantly agreed.

One Month Later

GROVE Since I spoke to you last, we've made several agreements with Candy. She's upset that Betty is overweight and does not try to look nice. She's also upset that Betty's not interested in men and never has sex. Candy says things like, "I'm horny!

You can't get a man with a body like this!" and, "When I was in charge, we didn't have a weight problem." We told Candy that we would help her with the weight problem and the man problem if she would make some agreements with us. The terms were: that she not do anything to endanger the son, that she not do anything to harm their body, and that she not do anything that's against the law. Candy was upset about these requests, because she knew it meant not going out of the house at night anymore, but she did agree.

HALEY   That's good, because I think you're right—she's neglecting the boy by leaving him at home alone at night. Does the son know about Candy?

GROVE   Now that Candy's not going out at night, what she does do is get up and wander around the house, smoke Betty's cigarettes, and rearrange things. Betty gets up in the morning and finds things moved around, and this is driving her crazy. Anyway, if the son happens to be up at night when Candy is up, Candy says she just ignores him. She doesn't say anything to him. Candy says the son doesn't know about her. The fascinating thing is that Candy made these agreements with us because she said the son was partly her responsibility. We asked her what did she mean by that, and she told a story of how the boy was conceived. She said that Betty picked this man up at a bar one night, and that Candy convinced Betty to sleep with him. Betty didn't want to spend the night with the man, and Candy did, and Candy says she talked Betty into it. That was the night the son was conceived. His conception was a product of both personalities.

HALEY   Isn't that something!

GROVE   Now listen to this. Candy said Betty was not aware of her, Candy's, influence on the decision to sleep with the man! Candy was influencing Betty's behavior outside of Betty's awareness. In fact, the boy was born when Betty was 22 years old. Betty says she got rid of Candy when Betty was 18. Now it sounds like Candy never really left. She's been looking in on Betty all along!

HALEY   You're still in a situation where Candy knows what Betty's doing, but Betty does not know what Candy's doing?

GROVE   When Candy's in charge of the body, Betty does not know what Candy's doing. Betty said that until she was age 18, she could become Candy at will, and she was aware of what Candy was doing. When she was 18, Betty got married, and she decided she did not need Candy anymore. At that point she stopped becoming Candy voluntarily. Now it looks like Betty just thinks she got rid of Candy when she was 18, but that Candy never really went away. Since then, Betty has been unaware of what Candy does. She has amnesia for what happens when Candy's in charge. That's the scary thing. I'm thinking that if we could just get Betty back to the point where she was before she was 18, when she could be aware of what Candy was doing, we would solve the amnesia problem. We're trying to get Betty to agree to having that as a goal. The problem is that Betty wants to just get rid of Candy, and we're trying to get the two to cooperate with each other.

HALEY   According to Erickson, that's typical. The personality that is unaware of the other is terrified of meeting the other personality. Imagine learning there might be another personality inside of you, taking over your body!

GROVE   With Betty, she's already aware that Candy exists, but she wants to get rid of her. One problem which I'm not sure how to handle is Betty's explanation for why Candy is around right now. Betty's really struggling with the question of why her mother was so abusive to her. Betty thinks her mother hated her. Betty's not sure what her own attitude toward her mother should be, if she should hate her for what happened or if she has to love her because she's her mother. Betty has this expectation that she's going to resolve something about her mother, and she's tying that in to why Candy is around right now.

Even Candy says that one reason why she, Candy, can take over at night is because Betty's exhausting herself thinking about her mother. Candy can take over because Betty is so tired. I need some plan for how to help Betty with her past. I'm not sure how to handle that or how to tie that into what's happening with Candy right now.

HALEY   Betty acts like there's something from her past to get rid of, but she doesn't act like she knows what it is. Does Betty think that if she could be aware of Candy that would resolve whatever the problem is with her mother?

GROVE   That's a good question. We haven't asked that. We did ask Candy, if Betty resolved these issues about her mother, would she, Candy, then go away. Candy said "no." But I didn't think of the idea that if Betty could know what Candy's doing, then that would help resolve these other issues.

HALEY   If you think of this as Betty producing Candy originally because her mother mistreated her, then you could think that Betty doing something now in relation to Candy might also resolve whatever issue she still has with her mother. Erickson had a procedure that you might try with these two. He tried to introduce the personalities to each other a little bit at a time. He had a way of doing that by having them see each other just for a moment in a mirror.

GROVE   I don't understand. Have Betty see Candy in a mirror, you mean?

HALEY   You start by having Betty look in a mirror. Then you have Candy take over. But before Candy takes over completely, there will be a slight delay. There will be a moment when Betty will see Candy in the mirror. Then you keep repeating that procedure over and over, trying to increase Betty's tolerance of Candy and her ability to see what Candy's doing when Candy's in charge. The goal would be that by the end of the session Betty would know what Candy's doing when Candy takes over.

GROVE   This is a procedure that would get Betty back to what she could do before she tried to get rid of Candy?

HALEY   That's right. Explain to Betty that if she could see what Candy was doing, then Candy couldn't go out at night without Betty knowing what was going on. Right now it's the other way around. Candy knows what Betty's doing, but Betty doesn't know what Candy's doing.

GROVE   What about the idea of getting the two to communicate directly with each other? We talked about a procedure for Candy to take over the hand, and then the two could communicate with each other by Candy writing and Betty talking.

HALEY   Right. But even if they could do that, Betty could still have the problem of Candy taking over the whole body, and Betty not knowing what Candy is doing. To eliminate the amnesia, you're after the goal of Betty being aware of what Candy's doing when Candy's in control. One procedure I know of involves using a mirror.

GROVE   Erickson used that in order to have them be aware of what each other is doing?

HALEY   Right. Erickson said it's like a kind of death for the dominant personality to be aware of the other personality.

GROVE   Well, in this case Betty was once able to have the experience of being aware of Candy when Candy was in charge. Our problem is getting Betty to draw on how she did that before.

HALEY   Sure. If she could do it before, she can do it again.

GROVE   One of the things I'm struggling with is that we are encouraging Betty to keep Candy, but Betty wants to get rid of Candy. She thinks that if she resolves these issues about her mother then Candy will be gone.

HALEY   I think you have to say to Betty that there are two problems. One is resolving the issues about her mother, and the other is learning that Candy's not so frightening.

GROVE   I could say to Betty that maybe Candy will go away, and maybe she won't. One issue between Betty and Candy is that Betty restricts herself in a lot of ways Candy doesn't. Candy's very assertive and doesn't allow herself to be pushed around. She cares about her appearance and wants to have relationships with men. To get rid of Candy would mean getting rid of all of that. Betty's very unassertive. She gets dominated by her sister and lets her son get away with murder.

HALEY You could persuade Betty that maybe Candy would be less active if Betty would pretend to be Candy. She could wear makeup like Candy, dress like Candy, and begin to do things that Candy does.

GROVE That's a great idea! You know one problem for me is that these two are so fascinating, and the ideas we discuss are so interesting that it's easy for me to lose sight of what would really be helpful for them.

HALEY I think anything you do that helps her to not have any more amnesia will be very helpful. If that means talking about two personalities, or her past with her mother, or seeing someone else in the mirror, then you should go along with that. She shouldn't be appearing in bars at night and not knowing how she got there.

GROVE Right. Betty keeps bringing up new things that she's had amnesia for. She says, "When I wake up in the morning, I'm so tired and exhausted. It's like I didn't sleep at all." Apparently it doesn't occur to Betty that she really isn't sleeping! She also told how she found her car parked in a place where she did not park it, with additional mileage ticked off. I think you're right; I'll settle for anything we can do that will get rid of the amnesia.

HALEY How old is Candy?

GROVE I'm not sure. We haven't asked her that question. Betty is 35, but we haven't asked Candy how old she is.

HALEY Candy came when Betty was 13?

GROVE She came when Betty was 13. Betty says she got rid of

Candy when she got married at age 18, but then she also said that when she got divorced at age 21, she thinks Candy was active then too. Even though she says she got rid of Candy at age 18, when she looks back on her life there are events after she was 18 that she suspects Candy is responsible for.

HALEY   I was thinking that if Candy doesn't know how to properly treat the son, it may be because she herself is a teenager and unable to supervise another teenager. Candy's acting like a teenager.

GROVE   Well that's true, but she's cooperating with the agreements she made with us. She no longer goes out at night. She just gets up at night and wanders around the house.

HALEY   I think what would help would be two things. First, to have a two- or three-hour session where you patiently work with them getting Betty to be more and more aware of Candy, while Candy takes over the body. Second, have a session where the two of them communicate with each other in your presence. If when she was younger Betty was aware of what Candy did while Candy was in the body, then Betty could probably do it again for you now pretty easily. I think Betty must be avoiding Candy.

GROVE   I think that must be true. There must be something she's avoiding.

HALEY   Betty may be afraid that if she were aware of Candy when Candy's in charge, then whatever she's avoiding would become apparent to her.

GROVE   To set that mirror procedure up, what would you tell Betty?

HALEY   I would set it up with Candy. Tell Candy you want her to introduce herself to Betty a little bit at a time, so Betty won't be afraid of her. Tell Candy you're going to have Betty look into a mirror, and you want her, Candy, to take over for just a moment, and then go away, so Betty can just catch a glimpse of her. Tell Candy you want her to keep repeating that over and over, staying in charge a little bit longer each time, until Betty can handle really taking a good look at her.

GROVE OK, I understand. You know, I think you're right about Betty avoiding something about Candy. When we had Candy come the first time, and write for us, Betty didn't want to see what Candy wrote. Also, before we brought Candy in, Betty was very concerned about whether she would know what Candy might say if Candy did come. We told Betty she would know or not know whatever she was comfortable knowing or not knowing. She ended up having total amnesia for everything Candy said that day. It looks like there's something Betty's avoiding about Candy.

HALEY She doesn't want to face Candy. It might be very hard for her to see Candy in the mirror. I would emphasize to Candy that you don't want her to frighten Betty.

GROVE With the handwriting procedure, where we try to get them to communicate with each other, we're trying to do anything that will get an interchange between the two of them. That might take some patience also.

HALEY You need a way for the two to communicate that Betty can do without being afraid. You could do a step-by-step procedure with that. You could start by having Candy write only what Betty asks her to write. Then you could go on to having Betty ask questions of Candy and having Candy respond only to Betty's questions and not say anything more. That way Candy would be cooperating with Betty and Betty would be less afraid. Eventually Candy can say to Betty whatever is on her mind. It's all going to take some patience. You could also ask Betty to pretend to be Candy. Ask her what she would look like, what she would wear.

GROVE Anything to help Betty be less afraid. Right now, Betty struggles to keep Candy away, then when she goes to sleep she's exhausted mentally and Candy takes advantage of that. Betty doesn't even allow Candy to look in on her and I think it's because she's afraid that if she let Candy look in, Candy would take over the whole body.

HALEY If Betty's in charge, does Candy know what Betty's doing?

GROVE I think sometimes she does. But Betty's struggling to keep Candy completely out.

HALEY If Candy only takes over when Betty sleeps, what's the logical thing to do on that?

GROVE What's your idea?

HALEY If Betty has a theory that sleep is an inactive state that makes her vulnerable to Candy, then I would educate her about sleep. Tell her sleep is not a time when you are relaxed and vulnerable, it's a time when your mind is active and clearing itself. That's why you have dreams. Sleep is an active state.

GROVE If we tell her that, wouldn't that be a way of helping Betty eliminate Candy? This is where I go back and forth. Should the goal be to eliminate Candy or to get the two of them to cooperate with each other?

HALEY Telling her about sleep is not trying to eliminate Candy. You're just trying to get Betty to feel comfortable about going to sleep at night. You would still have to get them to get acquainted with each other and to communicate with each other. Betty just wouldn't feel so vulnerable about going to sleep.

GROVE I understand. I think it's going to be tough to persuade Betty to stop trying to get rid of Candy. We'll have to convince her that Candy is an important part of her.

HALEY You know, I don't think Erickson ever tried to persuade the primary personality that it should know about the others. Getting acquainted with the other personalities happened with opposition from the primary personality because it was afraid. The primary personality was scared that if the other personality ever took over, that would be it. It would be gone. Erickson had a great case of a woman who had a dual personality. He said it took over one year of very patient work with the total cooperation from the secondary personality to get them introduced to each other. Once he got them past that, he then got them cooperating with each other, and he got them to have fun by playing tricks on people. Erickson arranged for them to have a date with a nice young man, and they played tricks on the poor guy. They would switch while he was dancing with them. One minute he'd be dancing with one girl, and the next minute he'd be dancing with another. It was the same girl, but also different. They had a great time confusing that poor young man. Erickson got them to have fun with each other like that, and that's how they could collaborate with each other. He made it an advantage to be two different people. I would tell Betty that she has a special ability that other people don't have.

GROVE That's great. With Betty, I think you're right; she's afraid Candy will take over completely. That's a terrible fear to have to live with.

HALEY It sure is. Especially if Candy doesn't behave herself.

After this consultation, the therapist and I conducted three consecutive sessions with Betty in which, to our astonishment, rapid and dramatic changes occurred. In the first session, we planned to frame Candy's presence in a positive light, and to set the goal with both personalities of communicating directly with each other. As a first step toward this goal, we used this session to get the two to communicate through the therapist. The therapist asked Betty if she had any questions she wished the therapist to ask Candy or if she had any agreements she wished to propose to Candy. We asked Candy the same questions. Betty's main question to Candy was why she wanted to pick up men at bars. Candy's response was "Because it's fun, and I'm horny!"

In an earlier session, Betty claimed she had "created Candy." In this interview, we framed Betty's capacity to create Candy as a "special ability." This was a powerful idea for Betty. She responded, "I never thought of Candy in that way. I always thought of her as my bad side." The therapist reiterated that Candy's presence represented a "special ability" and that, instead of trying to get rid of Candy, she should accept her. Betty was surprisingly agreeable to this.

We then set two goals with Betty. The first goal would be for Betty to be able to look in on Candy if Candy were in charge of the body, as she was able to do when she was a teenager. Betty understood this completely. The second goal was for Betty and Candy to learn to communicate directly with each other and to compromise on their differences. Betty asked how she could communicate with Candy directly, and the therapist explained she had a method that she would show her in the next session. The therapist also set both of these goals with Candy and explained to Candy that Betty would need Candy's assistance to accomplish this. Candy was agreeable.

One week later Betty arrived at the session with a completely new appearance. She was wearing her hair in a new style, was wearing contact lenses instead of glasses, and was wearing makeup for the first time since the therapist had known her. Betty explained, "We're compromising." Before we had a chance to work with them in a session, Candy had introduced herself to Betty on her own, and the two had already begun communicating and compromising. We had not discussed any procedure to either one of them for how they might accomplish this. What was truly fascinating was that they invented a method on their own using a mirror, similar to what Haley had described to me as Erickson's procedure. Betty explained, "For three nights in a row, when I went to bed I concentrated on Candy. I wanted her to come, but not to take over. On the third night, I dreamt that I got in front of a full-length mirror and saw Candy in the mirror. That is how we talked to each other."

Betty then described the compromises she and Candy had made: "We agreed that if I wear makeup, change my hair style, lose weight, and wear contacts, Candy will not go out at night or get up at night and move things around the house. One area we're stuck on is men. Candy still wants to go to bars and pick up red-necks!" Betty then stated that now that she had met and talked with Candy, she felt much more secure, and had removed all the bells from her doors.

I now had no doubt that the goal of having the two collaborate on how to share their body was correct. The therapist complimented Betty for having the courage to face Candy and explained that we would like to have the two of them continue their discussions in the session. We then brought Candy in the room and talked with her. Candy corroborated everything that Betty had said and agreed to communicate with Betty in the session.

The therapist then helped the two execute an automatic writing approach that Haley had explained to me in an earlier consultation. Candy went into the writing hand, and Betty was in charge of the rest of the body. The two communicated, with Betty talking and Candy writing. It was an extraordinary session. Their conversation centered on their disagreement about men. Betty did not want to get involved with a man, and Candy insisted she was "horny" and needed to have sex. The two resembled a mother and a teenage daughter. Candy was a rebellious teenager, trying to make her mother more youthful, and Betty was trying to set limits on an out-of-control daughter. The session ended with no compromise being found. We suggested that they continue their discussions. It was in this session that Candy revealed her age to be 17.

The next session one week later was no less extraordinary. Betty came with yet another dramatic change in appearance. She again was wearing makeup but now she had an entirely new hair style and color. She explained that this was her natural color. She said dramatically, "We decided that for me to become me, I can no longer hide under hair color, or weight. For me to become me, I have to go back to the way I was originally." Betty's personality was changing. She was more assertive and self-assured. She said that she was starting to blurt out things that Candy would say.

After my last consultation with Haley, I was convinced that there was something about Candy that Betty was avoiding. In the previous session, I had hoped this would come out when the two talked to each other in the session, but it did not. In this session I had the therapist ask Betty directly if she thought there might be something about Candy or something that Candy might know that she, Betty, might be avoiding. Betty said there was and that she had dreamt about it the very night before this session.

Betty said Candy had told her to, "Go back to the night you made me. All of your answers are there." Betty then relived a terrible night when she was 13 years old. Her mother came home drunk. Betty and her brother struggled to get her upstairs and into bed. At some point during the struggle, the mother hit her head and was knocked unconscious. When the mother came to, she was out of her mind. She threw a chair so hard at Betty that when it missed and struck the wall it stuck in the wall. She then grabbed Betty by the throat and tried to strangle her. Betty said, "She looked at me with hateful eyes and said she would see me dead before the night was through." Finally the two siblings got their mother put to bed. Betty spent the remainder of the night sitting behind her bedroom door holding a baseball bat. What disturbed Betty the most was not the beatings or the actual physical abuse. She was most upset by her mother's hateful gaze and the idea that her mother hated her.

After Betty had told us this terrible story, we brought Candy into the room to get her account. Candy explained emphatically that she was not going to leave Betty alone until Betty had faced that night. We asked Candy what would happen to her now that Betty had relived that night. Candy said she would not take over the body. She said, "I will be a voice in the back of Betty's mind." The session ended with both myself and the therapist astounded and pleased at the progress the two had made. I was also very concerned that Betty continued to be tortured by the idea that her mother hated her. I felt we needed to find some way to reframe the mother's behavior so Betty would at least begin to doubt that her mother hated her.

The next session was six weeks later. Betty again surprised us with the progress she had made. After her last session, she went on a mission and interviewed several of her relatives, including a maternal uncle, about her parents. She discovered that she greatly resembled her natural father. Betty's father had died unexpectedly when Betty was six years old. Her uncle told her that her mother was very angry at the father for dying on her and leaving her to raise three children all by herself, with no money. Betty concluded that since she looked like her father, when her mother looked at her with "hateful eyes," she was not seeing Betty, but Betty's father. Betty decided her mother hated her father, not her. This was a better reframing than I could ever have thought of. It gave Betty great peace of mind. After she realized this, she went and visited her mother's grave for the first time since her mother died ten years earlier. Betty then informed us of several other changes she had initiated. She had gone on a weight loss program and had found a boyfriend. She explained that she and Candy had reached a compromise on men: Betty would find a man to be friends with but not have sex for a while. This was a true shift for both personalities. Betty had also enrolled in a study program to get her high school degree. The changes in her personality that we had observed in the previous session had persisted.

Betty's growing confidence was also reflected in her setting more effective limits with her son. One interesting note: Early in the therapy Betty struggled with the question of why Candy was so active at this time. The night Betty created Candy, Betty had just turned 13; at the time of the therapy, Betty's son had just turned 13.

Follow-Up

Betty came in for one last session two months later. She was continuing with the changes she had described in the previous session. She still had her man friend, with whom she was not having sex. She had taken and passed her test for her high school diploma, and had enrolled in technical school for the upcoming semester. She was also continuing on her weight loss program. Of all of the changes, the weight loss was perhaps the most important. In one of the early sessions, Candy explained that Betty had gained all the weight for two reasons. First, it angered her mother because it made Betty less desirable to men when her mother wanted to prostitute her. Also, and no less important, on the night Betty's mother came home drunk and tried to kill her, Betty said she weighed only about 100 pounds. She said she was not strong enough to defend herself against her mother's attacks. Betty's weight was her protection. For a woman with this history, losing weight was very significant.

Regarding Candy, Betty had some very interesting things to report. Betty had not had any further episodes of amnesia, and she was certain Candy was not taking over their body anymore. On occasion, however, Betty found herself responding to situations in a way Candy would. For example, if her sister tried to dominate her, Betty would "feel" Candy's presence, and she would assert herself and say exactly what Candy would want her to say. I privately took this to indicate that, as promised, Candy had remained as a voice in the back of Betty's mind. The two were sharing the same body and compromising.

The therapist made an additional follow-up with Betty by phone approximately one year later. At that time Betty was continuing her education and had had no further episodes of amnesia.

Therapists dealing with cases of multiple personality should note that the success of this case could be said to be determined not only by the skill of therapist and supervisor but also by a particular way of thinking about this problem derived from Milton H. Erickson. Additional personalities are not thought of as dissociated states to be merged. Instead they are seen as helpers who can collaborate and make a positive contribution to the life of the total person.

NOTES

CHAPTER 1: EMPOWERING FAMILIES

1. See Cloé Madanes, *Behind the One-Way Mirror*, San Francisco: Jossey-Bass, 1984, pp. 31–58.
2. See Cloé Madanes, *Sex, Love, and Violence*, New York: Norton, 1990, pp. 51–63.
3. See Madanes, *Behind the One-Way Mirror*.

CHAPTER 2: MARITAL CONTRACTS

1. Over the past decade, many brief therapy approaches have abandoned the ideas that symptoms have a stabilizing function within the client's social group and the concept of reciprocity among couples (e.g., R. Fisch, J. Weakland, and L. Segal, *The Tactics of Change*, San Francisco: Jossey-Bass, 1986; S. de Shazer, *Keys to Solution in Brief Therapy*, New York: Norton, 1985; M. White, "Negative explanation, restraint and double description: A template for family therapy," *Family Process*, 25(2), 169–184, 1986). We here re-assert the importance of these ideas, particularly in relation to the social unit on which the therapy will directly focus.

2. See Jay Haley, *Ordeal Therapy*, San Francisco: Jossey-Bass, 1984, pp. 121–125.

CHAPTER 4: INFIDELITY

1. Personal communication from Richard Stuart to Jay Haley.
2. See Jay Haley, *Uncommon Therapy*, New York: Norton, 1973, p. 247.

CHAPTER 5: ABUSE

1. Personal communication from Charles Fulweiler to Jay Haley.
2. See Madanes, *Sex, Love, and Violence*, pp. 51–64.
3. See Sigmund Freud, "The aetiology of hysteria (1896)," in *The Standard Edition of the Complete Psychological Works of Sigmund Freud*, volume III, pp. 191–221, London: Hogarth Press.
4. The literature on multiple personality disorder is filled with examples of therapy approaches which assume the client must have been abused and focus on recovering memories of past abuse. See, e.g., F. W. Putnam, *Diagnosis and Treatment of Multiple Personality Disorder*, New York: Guilford, 1989, pp. 218–252.
5. See Madanes, *Sex, Love, and Violence*.
6. This case, with additional theoretical discussion, also appears in D. Grove, "Ericksonian approaches to multiple personality disorder," *Journal of Family Psychotherapy*, in press.

Index

201